Fading Splendour?

Fading Splendour?

JOHN FINNEY

DARTON·LONGMAN+TODD

First published in 2000 by
Darton, Longman and Todd Ltd
1 Spencer Court
140–142 Wandsworth High Street
London SW18 4JJ

ISBN 0–232–52286–3

A catalogue record for this book is available from the British Library.

Designed by Sandie Boccacci
Phototypeset in 10/13^1/$_4$pt Palatino by Intype London Ltd
Printed and bound in Great Britain by
Redwood Books, Trowbridge, Wiltshire

Contents

Preface

This book is about those disturbances in the Church which we call renewals. Down the ages there have always been periods when new light seems to have been given. Today is a day of renewals – different from each other in form and extent, but every one playing their part in quickening the whole.

This book looks at history to get a perspective on the present. I am well aware that this is a dangerous enterprise, for history is not well regarded in our post-modern days. Nevertheless, outside academic circles, there has never been a greater interest in the past. Tradition can be a keel without which the boat drifts aimlessly.

Two quotations illustrate the difficulty in a book of this kind:

> History repeats itself
> historians repeat each other. (Philip Guedalla)

> History does not repeat itself
> historians repeat each other. (Arthur Balfour)

The first lines of both statements are reconcilable for we find that while today may not be an exact replay of the past, it certainly resonates with the past.

However, I find their agreed statement about historians to be depressing. My debt to historians and sociologists is immense and if I have misinterpreted their work I can only offer my apologies.

My thanks to all who made this book a possibility, not least to my wife who bore with my absences. Above all my thanks to

Almighty God, who showed me that there is nothing about retirement in the Bible.

JOHN FINNEY
April 2000

Introduction

WHY DO CUPS OF TEA ALWAYS BECOME LUKEWARM?

The second law of thermodynamics is depressing. It says that
things wear out, become more alike, distinctions disappear. Put
an ice cube into a cup of hot tea – the ice melts, the tea becomes
cool: you never find the reverse – a block of ice forming in a
hot cup of tea. Things tend to become more bland, less different,
more ordinary.

Does a similar law also operate in our lives together? Whether
we think about politics or the life of the Church, or any new
project within a community, is there a tendency for differences
to become less pronounced? With the passage of time does the
more extreme move nearer to the routine, and the exciting settle
down into the dull? Some think so. An ex-New Church leader
speaks of his disillusionment:

> We started this brand new thing which was going to be
> the best thing since sliced bread and that began to show the
> normal weaknesses that any organisation would do. We
> became institutionalised, like everything – it happens to
> everything in the end.[1]

Newman said wearily that 'every great movement seems to
start with a prophet and end up with a policeman'.

Certainly in the political field the same law of entropy seems
to apply. Idealisms turn to dust or worse as time passes. As
Tillich says, 'If a revolutionary movement becomes victorious,
then it loses its character of a sect and becomes a church, with

a hierarchy, with authority and suppression'.[2] Communism attracted many who wanted to change the world for the good of the great mass of people – and ended as a political system which could only be totalitarian or inept. Many politicians with high motives find that the grind of daily work, the brickbats thrown by those who disagree and the intractability of organisations like the civil service means that their aspirations first become blunted and then turn to a bitter cynicism.

As we shall see, the periodic renewals which touch the Church have been indispensable to her vitality. But despite this renewals have tended to fade. Although ideals are often high and faith abundant the difficulties that renewals face as the years pass can sap enthusiasm and degenerate into factionalism. In this book we shall be looking at some of the ways in which this can happen – and what, if anything, can be done about it. The spiritual question at the heart of the matter is: *'Does God always expect us to be disappointed?'*

The argument put forward in this book is that certain patterns can be discerned in the New Testament and the life of the Church. We shall glance at other fields where humans act together in political and community life and at the experience of other faiths and sects, for we need to see whether what happens within the Church takes place elsewhere. However, we shall stick mainly with the Christian Church. We shall see that there have been wave after wave of 'renewal' during those two thousand years; indeed the New Testament can be seen as a renewal movement within the Jewish faith of its day. We shall look in more detail at three such movements after the New Testament to see what they can teach us. Although we shall not subject modern renewal movements to the same treatment there are constant references to the history which is in the making today.

At the outset, however, I do not think that we need to be disheartened by the apparent inevitability of 'decline'. There are two reasons, both of which have to do with the being of God Almighty.

First, God is our Creator. Therefore he well knows the human heart and its needs and how we relate to each other and what happens when we work together. So if we find that there is something in the social life of humans which inevitably means that organisations become institutionalised, that renewals become 'cooler', that hopes fade, then this is to be accepted as part of the human lot rather than grumbled about and fought against. If we accept this we will work with the grain of human existence and not against it. Further we will not be discouraged when it happens and learn both to see what is good in the process and how to manage it. If not, we shall be sucked into disillusionment ('Why has God let us down?'), denial ('Things are really just as good as they used to be') or even despair ('It's all my fault'). It is to help people who feel like this that this book has been written.

Second, God is a God of patterns. Things happen in accordance with an elegant plan, traces of which we may glimpse from time to time. Our forefathers talked about 'Providence' to describe this ordering of the universe. Modern talk about chaos theory and fractals should not blind us to the majestic routine of creation. Every snowflake is different in pattern from every other – yet there is a basic hexagonal structure to them all. This is not to suggest a divine determinism, for modern science also suggests to us that the universe does not run on predetermined railway lines – God's plan can be infinitely changing yet totally secure.

It is the same with history. The past does not repeat itself, but it can tell us how human beings have reacted with each other and their environment. Whether they are diplomats in their chancelleries or peasants in their hovels, the way in which they talked and lived and died can be more than illustrative. The French Revolution is more than the story of one European nation: it can teach us about revolutionary movements – how they start, develop and can end by betraying themselves.

The God who orders the universe uses patterns in which we can see him at work. He never repeats himself exactly, because the raw material, whether magnetic fields or human beings, is never identical.

The impact of some form of spiritual renewal on the life of a church or a denomination or a nation does not have random, unpredictable consequences. Other churches at other times have had similar experiences: we can learn from them. But this does not mean that we should copy them. At times people have tried to replicate the Reformation or one of the American revivals, or even the New Testament. Local church leaders have sometimes tried to copy another church and hoped they would see the same results: they have admired the story of its life and wanted *their* church to be the same. That way lies frustration and disenchantment. Every revival is newly minted coin. It is different from any that has ever been before or that will ever come after. We can learn from it, but we can never duplicate it. The Holy Spirit does his work with human beings in their context – and both are unique. Besides, if all we had to do was to copy, where would be the faith, where the excitement of treading new paths? Where could we learn the ways of a trail-blazing God?

This applies as much to the New Testament as to any other story of renewal. To follow slavishly what is perceived to be that pattern will also lead to dissatisfaction. Corinth is not the same as Coventry or Canberra or Cincinnati. We should learn from but not strive to produce a clone of the New Testament. Anyway who would want to be a leader in the fractious, sinful, divided and heretical church in Corinth?

This does not mean we should ignore what has happened in the past. It is not enough to say 'The Spirit blows where it wills', for the Holy Spirit does not work arbitrarily. In Genesis 1 he is shown as making patterns out of the primeval chaos, ordering the firmament. The creative activity of God is never capricious, following one set of rules at one time and then changing them. We may have difficulty in discerning the course of that activity at times and in seeing why one particular cause has certain effects but there is an underlying orderliness. This is the basis of all science and of all life. If God switched gravity off from time to time the universe would be chaotic – and non-existent.

Scientists seek to discern the footsteps of the Creator: Christians should also seek the patterns of the Creator in the lives of the people he made and in the life of his Church.

It is that quest for patterns that this book is engaged in. In Chapter 1, I put before you a hypothesis. It is for you to test it: if it stands up to that inspection I hope that it will be helpful to all Christians and of direct help to Church leaders, whether they oversee a local church, a denomination or a Christian organisation.

A NEW PARADIGM?

That we should be seeking for the signs of the Holy Spirit at the beginning of a new millennium is particularly appropriate. As David Jones wrote, 'It is easy to miss Him at the turn of a civilisation'.[3]

We are looking at these matters from the perspective of the year 2000. We have to take into account the effect of that viewpoint, for we are at a crossroads in our thinking. Terms like modernism and post-modernism are tossed around, often too lightly, but they do represent something which we shall have to think about towards the end of the book when we consider what we can learn from our journey into the Christian past. We are not just pawing old bones for academic interest. We are doing so in order that within the Church we can better cope with 'renewals', with all that they have of the spiritual and the all-too-human.

David Bosch in *Transforming Mission* noted: 'Today there is a growing sense of disaffection with the Enlightenment and a quest for a new approach to an understanding of reality.'[4]

The idea of a 'paradigm shift' is a commonplace of modern thinking. It was coined by Thomas Kuhn[5] who was primarily interested in the history of science. He noticed that when a new scientific theory was first proposed it went through a pattern of rejection, resuscitation and finally acceptance. After it had become received wisdom things were never regarded in the same light again. Once Newton's views on gravity were accepted we never looked at the universe with the same eyes. A paradigm shift had taken place. The same is true in theology and, indeed, all the arts. After Augustine of Hippo things could never go back to how they were before he had written. The Reformation produced a new paradigm, as did biblical criticism. Like them or not, you cannot behave as though these things have never happened.

But there is a considerable difference between the arts and the sciences. Kuhn perceived that it is perfectly possible for different theologians (or artists, or politicians, or historians) to inhabit different paradigms. No scientist these days believes that the sun goes round the earth: he or she cannot go back to the time before Copernicus. But it is perfectly possible for different Christians to inhabit conflicting paradigms. Hans Kung points out that the medieval Roman Catholic paradigm is still vigorous in traditionalist Catholicism today, and the Protestant Reformation paradigm is still seen in some evangelical circles.

Later we shall have to look at the importance of the new outlooks for the mission of the Church. While it is common today to use the term 'paradigm', readers may be more comfortable in using the term 'belief system' as suggested by Hiebert.[6] That term suggests that there has to be a commitment of the will to the new way of thinking as well as an intellectual assent. This is certainly true of theology. Indeed it is also more true of science than is commonly believed, since, as Hiebert says, 'the personal attitude and commitment of the researcher cannot be expunged from his or her research'. It is doubtful if full objectivity is ever possible.

WHAT IS RENEWAL?

The very word 'renewal' is vastly difficult to define. Its meaning can be suggested these days by a series of names. Ivor Smith-Cameron suggests 'Taizé, Iona, Cerne Abbas, Greenbelt, Spring Harvest, the Ashram movement, Cursillo, Roots Groups and Christian Aid'.[7] While this is useful in indicating the sort of activity which is involved in renewal it does not define renewal itself.

We need to define the scale in which we are operating. Renewal can be spoken of as *individual* – someone is conscious of being touched by God and having a closer relationship with him. This is often fostered actively by churches which could be called 'traditional' Catholic or Protestant; but the church itself is not changed since they see themselves as in no need of reform. In this case renewal can only be on a personal, moral level. Renewal can also be *congregational* – a local church is 'renewed' and this changes its attitude to mission, its styles of worship, its organisational structure and much else. This can happen because of a desire by some for the local church to adapt to the modern world or to 'return to the Bible' or 'be open to the Spirit'. Finally, renewal can be *denominational* – where there are Church-wide changes such as those involved in the Reformation or Vatican II. This may stem from a wish to see the whole denomination 'like the New Testament church' or 'truly Catholic' or 'properly Pentecostal'. Usually whole churches only embark on this process when they can see that there is disaster ahead which requires drastic action.[8]

We need to distinguish the word 'renewal' from two other words. The first is *'reform'*. Reform has about it more of the deliberation of human beings than has renewal. It has to do with structures and with liturgies and procedures. It may well be very necessary at any level but it is not renewal, which presupposes more of the initiative of God.

On the other side we have to distinguish renewal from the word *'revival'*. This is essential since later we shall be looking at the American 'Revivals' of the eighteenth and nineteenth centuries and seeing what can be learnt from them. It is generally used as descriptive of a sovereign work of God in bringing people to repentance and faith, and such events as the Welsh Revival of 1905 and the Hebridean Revival of 1948 are cited.[9] In general usage, renewal is seen as less directly God's work and more under the control of individuals or churches.

There is undoubtedly a considerable overlap in the meanings

of 'reform', 'renewal' and 'revival'. They differ in the degree of human and divine activity. Reform is primarily a human exercise, albeit guided by God. Revival is a divine irruption, though using human agents. Renewal is in the middle – both divine and human.

One of the most thorough examinations of the word 'renewal' was carried out as long ago as 1955 by Visser d'Hooft, who was at that time the General Secretary of the World Council of Churches. In the Dale Lecture in Oxford he explained that he saw renewal as a continuous process rather than a single event. He quotes Luther: 'It is not yet done and accomplished, but it is going on. It is not the end but the way. It is not all glistening and shining but it is all being swept.' He then spells out six features of a God-inspired and healthy renewal:

1. It begins with an encounter between God and man, in which God takes the initiative.
2. It is based on hearing the Bible afresh.
3. There cannot be any renewal except through the Holy Spirit.
4. There must be repentance – 'a cutting away from ego-centricity and church-centredness to God's Kingdom'.[10]
5. It restores true fellowship. 'Koinonia belongs to the very nature of the Church and depends on the re-entry of the Church into the realm of the new creation.'
6. Renewal means that the message of the gospel is proclaimed both to the Church and to the world and that this is the normal work of the Church.

He ends with an important statement which we shall find is all too true about renewals:

> Every intervention of the Holy Spirit appears as a partial intervention and all true newness in the Church seems to lead a precarious existence. There is in the life of the Church in history no definitive renewal – no renewal which is not threatened by relapse – no reformation which is not followed by some form of deformation. But if we conclude

that therefore the situation of the Church is hopeless we are wholly at variance with the biblical view.

D'Hooft's comment about there being 'no definitive renewal' is something we shall see illustrated repeatedly in this book. There is no renewal which is normative and which can simply be copied. No church has got it right for all time and all places – and that applies to the New Testament Church as well as to the Church in every succeeding century. There are no 'laws of renewal' in the Bible which give us a blueprint for every situation. The Bible is both more profound and more subtle.

But even that excellent description of the nature of renewal does not give us a definition. Perhaps the word 'revitalisation' gives the meaning more accurately. Thus A.F.C. Wallace writes about both political and religious 'Revitalisation Movements', which are:

> revolutions, religious revivals, charismatic movements, sects and cargo cults, and reform, mass and social movements generally. Hence political manifestos such as the American Declaration of Independence and the French Declaration of the Rights of Man and the Citizen and Augustus's Res Gestae Divi Augusti.[11]

The meaning of renewal is like jelly: you can recognise it for what it is easily enough, but defining it is difficult. The best that can be offered is:

> A revitalisation of the life of an organisation or individual which revives what has become stale, reinvigorates what has become routine and opens up new possibilities. In religious matters it is partly the work of God and partly the work of human beings and can be distinguished both from reform and revival.

TRUTHS – OR HALF-TRUTHS?

It has become normal both in theology and in sociology to distinguish between the church and the sect. The former

describes a long-established organisation, often seen as hidebound with tradition, unable to adapt to a changing context
and with a hierarchical form of leadership. The sect is described
in terms of movement, dynamism, forward thinking and
progress. The designation is often its own value-judgement:
church – bad, sect – good.[12]

We need to be cautious of this polarisation (as of any attempt
in any walk of life to make extremes appear representative). It
can lead to too-ready categorisation and division where none
exists.

We shall now look at five distinctions which are commonly
drawn. But we do so in order to learn from them rather than
to adopt the black/white way in which they are often presented.
As we shall see, there is a spectrum between these pairs of
opposites, and it is in this spectrum that real churches and
real organisations lie. However, extremes can be instructive
provided we remember that they are the outer limits and not
an indication of normality.

Church	**Sect**
Cain	Abel
Priest	Prophet
Jerusalem	Galilee
Roman	Celtic
Church	Para-church

1. Cain/Abel

Here are two archetypes – Cain the farmer, Abel the hunter-
gatherer and herdsman. Abel and his successors to this day
have a more exciting job. Down the ages he has taken many
forms – the tribal warrior, the medieval knight, the Tudor
merchant-adventurer, the modern entrepreneur. He (it usually
is a he) is seen as the risk-taker, the explorer of new horizons.
By contrast, Cain's work is routine and dull – the agricultural
labourer who, in many parts of the world, still plods behind
the plough as he has done since prehistoric times.

The life of the sect can seem more exciting, more dynamic. Whether you are the trail-breaking leader or the excited follower the sect offers colour and life. You become part of a movement which has the world at its feet: today our group, tomorrow the planet. In the early 1900s there was much fervent talk in the missionary movement by those who computed that by the year 1950 all the world would have become Christian. In the early 1980s some in the House Church Movement[13] were saying the whole of England would be Christian by 2020 and the mainline denominations would be insignificant or dead. Such claims should not be derided as dishonest. Sects are often under attack (or perceive themselves to be) and while these claims may be no more than the ritual boasting of a warrior or the overblown claims of a get-rich-quick enterprise, it is often the motivational force which can inspire and encourage the morale of the faithful.

Cain may have been killed in the story but he won in the end. Growing crops produces food more efficiently than hunting or grazing animals. It was agriculture which meant that villages could be established since there was no longer any need to follow the wanderings of the wild animals. The villages became towns and made technological advance possible. It is upon Cain and his kind that our modern civilisation is based. The force was with him.

We must not be seduced by the glamour of Abel with his claim of new ideas, fresh things to do, more risks to take. He may be right but not necessarily so. Solomon asked for wisdom. It is the essential leadership gift. In New Testament terms it is the gift of 'discernment' – the ability to tell right from wrong and, possibly more important, the right path from the good one.[14] As Christ points out in Matthew 7:13, the attractive and popular is not always right: 'the road is hard that leads to life.'

2. Priest/Prophet

The contrast between the priest who is the keeper of the cultus and the freebooting prophet who proclaims the Word of the

Lord has been often made. Certainly in the Old Testament the distinction is plain. Generally the priest has the worst press and the Old Testament ends with a wholehearted condemnation in Malachi. Similarly in the New Testament it is the priests in their role as religious officials who are denounced by Jesus for their pettifogging rules, their blindness to the important issues, their lack of care for people, their unwillingness to see the truth.

The prophets had an awesome task – they are the Word-bearers. They are the ones who say, 'Thus saith the Lord'. Great is their condemnation if they get it wrong. But they were popular: there were groups of prophets and they had many followers, attracted by their forthrightness and excited by their message.

However, when we read in Acts that 'a great many of the priests became obedient to the faith'[15] we realise that there may be another side to the story. There were many priests who sincerely sought the Lord, just as there were many prophets who said 'Thus saith the Lord' falsely.[16] We do not hear much of what the priests thought about the prophets, though it is not difficult to guess – rabble-rousers, irresponsible, lacking in perspective, and, above all, failing to understand the daily pressures upon them, the priests.

In addition, there were some who spanned both roles. Jeremiah was a priest as well as a prophet. I wonder if some of the pressures he expresses with such evident pain were the love-hate feelings he had towards the religious instititution. I have met few church leaders who do not have an ambivalent view of the organisation in which they have their being. Indeed this may be a necessary stress. On the one hand there is a proper loyalty to the Church as an organisation, and on the other a longing for what the organisation should be and could be under the hand of God. Indeed a leader who does not experience this pressure may need to repent, for it may indicate either a supine acceptance of things as they are or an adolescent rejection and lack of concern for authority.

Supremely, Jesus Christ himself was both priest and prophet.

He was popularly believed to be a prophet: 'the crowds were saying, "This is the prophet Jesus from Nazareth in Galilee".'[17] But later reflection, above all by the writer of Hebrews, saw him also as a priest, not in the old Aaronic line, but in the even more ancient priesthood of Melchizedek. He did not need to 'stand day after day . . . offering again and again the same sacrifices'. Christ 'offered once for all time a single sacrifice for sins' – himself.[18] His words are prophetic, his actions priestly.

Therefore, although this prophet/priest contrast cannot be too closely drawn the distinction has its lessons. First, there was a lack of understanding between priest and prophet. Each thought they were doing the work of God – the priest by his regular, steady worship of God and the prophet by passing on the words which God had put in his mouth.[19] We shall find the same lack of understanding between the mendicant friars and the regular clergy in the Middle Ages and the parochial ministers and the wandering revivalists in nineteenth-century America.

This rift hid an even more basic difference in spiritual perception. For the priest God was the One who had to be worshipped in the traditional way in the usual place at the customary time. God was not in a hurry. The prophet, on the other hand, had a mouth scorched by the urgent fire of God[20] – the living God had met with him and he was under orders to unburden himself to the world. The priest worshipped a God who was transcendent and distant, the Creator and Sustainer. The prophet worshipped an immanent God, closer than a friend, who demanded that the Word was proclaimed.

Thirdly, the priest thought sacramentally: it was in and through *things* that God could be perceived – the ancient book, the Temple, the ritual. The prophet, however, was a man of words – spoken or written, the message had to be blazed abroad.

3. *Jerusalem/Galilee*

Ivor Smith-Cameron sees Jerusalem as:

> a place where the venerable tradition is maintained and
> lived out, a place of sacrament and prayer, a place of
> priesthood and ministry, a place of fellowship and worship,
> the honoured and hallowed place of pilgrimage and
> pastoral care.

On the other hand, Galilee is:

> Galilee of the Gentiles . . . where politics and religion are
> mixed inextricably. Galilee of the market-place.[21]

Jerusalem is seen as the place of rules and regulations, of careful
precision and ecclesiastical politics. Galilee is more involved
with the world, less churchy. It is the People of God in the
harsh suffering of 'real' life.

Further, it has to be said, Jerusalem is a better class of place.
Galilee was seen as provincial and crude. The bystander in
the High Priest's house immediately recognised Peter's local
dialect.[22] It grated on the sophisticated ears of the people of
Jerusalem. To them the Galileans were rough-and-ready folk.
They were ignorant village people, not educated city-dwellers
like themselves. Moreover, their religion was suspect because
in Galilee the Jews mixed with those of other faiths and cultures,
and so, Jerusalem reasoned, their faith had to be contaminated.

In addition, Jerusalem was the capital city. It was there the
influential lived and there the important decisions were made.
Above all it was not just the centre of politics and culture, it
was, in matters of religion, pre-eminent. At its heart was one
of the great wonders of its age – the Temple itself, the focus of
their faith, the abode of God. The disciples felt like country
yokels as they walked in a city of such splendour and significance.[23] To the high priests their message must have seemed
simplistic and lacking in theological nuances – a theology of
amateur laity not of priestly professionals.

The northerners from Galilee must have felt themselves

despised and mocked for their 'common' ways and their impure Aramaic speech. Outwardly expressed or not, this contempt corroded their self-confidence and made them feel socially inferior. It helps to explain their cowardice in Gethsemane in the same way that it was a factor in Peter's betrayal of Christ.

When we examine the different episodes of renewal we should not be blind to the impact of social distinctions. These factors often play a part. The Early Church itself was made up of the socially inferior: in 1 Corinthians 1:26–31 Paul teaches them to glory in the fact that God chose them, the 'low and despised', to be ahead of the wise and socially adept. We shall look at the Montanists, who were country people establishing a new movement when the strength of the contemporary Church was in the towns; many Christians regarded the movement as merely strange goings-on among rustic bumpkins.

Also there is often a difference between the vigour and thrust of those who are not in the centres of ecclesiastical and other forms of power and the caution of those who are. The priestly authorities in Jerusalem were desperately concerned that the commotion caused by this northern preacher should not lead to civil unrest and the intervention of the Romans – 'it is better to have one man die for the people than to have the whole nation destroyed'.[24] They had long since reached an accommodation with the occupying forces and they did not want some hothead to interfere. Like most ecclesiastical politicians they preferred the quiet backstairs way, which whispers the right thing in the right ear. In their considerable experience, shouting from the housetops achieved little except trouble.

The Jerusalem/Galilee distinction is about power and how it is handled and even subverted. Galilee portrays the pilgrim Church of ordinary people;[25] Jerusalem is the traditional Church of the movers and shakers. It is also about class and how different groups of people regard each other. In our thinking about renewal we shall often find these factors significant. The early Methodists, for example, were viewed as uneducated folk, not fit for elegant eighteenth-century society.

4. Roman/Celtic

1997 marked the fourteen-hundredth anniversary of the coming of St Augustine to evangelise England and also of the death of St Columba. The celebrations often led to a raw distinction being drawn between the cool, over-precise authoritarian and not very successful Romans and the human, flexible, inclusive, democratically inclined and evangelistically successful Celts. I have argued elsewhere[26] that this is a greatly overdrawn distinction and I have poured gentle scorn on the myths of what I christened the 'Green Industry', which sees the Celts as the first politically correct people on the planet.

Nevertheless, even if we are suspicious of the cavalier misuse of history which sometimes infects the study of this period, there was one genuine and very significant distinction. The Romans were centralisers and unifiers. Gregory the Great was a remarkable man and, standing as he did in the ruins of the Roman Empire, he wanted a single Church, strong and united enough to be able to bring to Europe a peace which it had not known for two hundred years. In order for his vision to become reality he needed:

(a) to ensure that the remaining pagan lands were evangelised as soon as possible;

(b) to make Rome once again the centre of the Church in a time when there were many centrifugal forces;

(c) to give a common focus to the Church by enforcing a unity of liturgy and practice.

The Celts, on the other hand, were notoriously uncentralised. Their only centres were places like Iona, Lindisfarne and Luxueil where major monasteries were established for both retreat and evangelistic outreach. Their practices were, to the neat-minded Romans, blatantly irregular, and their liturgy varied greatly from place to place. They could be untidy and irresponsible in their frequent wanderings (as even their own abbots admitted), though these peregrinations were often extremely fruitful.

In the short term the centralisers won, though it took many centuries before all Gregory's aims were achieved. The liturgy was codified, the practices of the Church became uniform, Rome and the Pope became the centre of authority. In the chaos of seventh-century Europe there was probably no alternative, but in the long term it stored up trouble. First the Eastern Churches broke away, and then the Reformers objected to the straitjacket into which people had been strapped.

We shall see in this book the difficulties which come from the desire of those pursuing renewal to maintain what is perceived to be its original fire and purity through increasingly autocratic means. In the short term it can appear to work, but only at the cost of stifling new life. Sooner or later the dam bursts.

5. *Church/Para-church*

The Christian Church has included, certainly from the time of the rise of the monastic movement in the fourth century, elements which are not in themselves a church but are dependent upon it. These 'para-church' organisations can be seen in the religious orders, missionary societies and in the myriad of different groupings for prayer, social work, evangelism and so on which exist.[27]

The para-church groups are examples of the voluntaryist principle we shall look at later. They can be quicker off the mark, more experimental, less concerned with the opinions of others than the Church itself. They are also more fragile, less balanced and fall more easily into error.

As we shall see, many of these para-church groups have been extremely influential in changing the life of the whole Church. Many renewals give birth to such groups and are supported by them. Thus in the UK, the first letter of the alphabet alone covers Acorn Christian Healing Trust, Affirming Catholicism, Anglican Renewal Ministries and the Arthur Rank Centre.

In church growth teaching, para-church is sometimes equated

with 'sodality' as opposed to 'modality', which describes the ordered, settled, pastoral life of the Church.

TIME

One factor that we shall always encounter is the importance of the passage of time. Renewals change, sometimes slowly, but often with great rapidity. We shall look at the Reformation, which still affects the Western Church four hundred years later. But that is exceptional. In examining the monastic movements and the modern charismatic movements we shall see that a decade is a long time. The New Testament itself faced the question of time – when was Christ coming back? As David Bosch says:

> Paul can simultaneously hold together two seemingly opposite realities: a fervent longing for the breaking in of the future reign of God; and a preoccupation with missionary outreach, the building up of communities of faith in a hostile world, and practice of a new societal ethic ... most Christian groups find it impossible to live creatively in the abiding tension between the penultimate and the ultimate.[28]

The Christian faith is a historical faith and the Church grapples with the passage of time most vividly when encountering renewals. The sorts of question we shall encounter repeatedly are:

- Have the sensations of God which we once experienced gone for ever?
- How quickly can the institution of the Church change or do we have to begin all over again?

And perhaps most sadly,

- Does time always corrupt the early enthusiasms, the ideals, the visions?

PRACTICAL THEOLOGY

An apologia for a theology which seeks to be applied in the world, and for experiences which seek a theology, does not have to be made so forcefully these days. The need for an 'earthed theology' is clear to all, and the divergence between 'academic theology' and the life of the Church in the world is possibly not as painfully obvious as was the case some years ago.

Practical theology is the thinking of the Church transmuted into the action of the Church. As Karl Barth said:

> Practical theology ... is theology in transition to the practical work of the community ... Practical theology is studied in order to seek and to find, to learn and to practice, this speech that is essential to the proclamation of the community in preaching and teaching, in worship and evangelisation.[29]

But it is not a one-way street from academia to the 'church on the ground'. It is also the ordinary church members posing to the scholar the questions which need an answer. Sometimes theology has sought to answer questions which no one was asking, and too much action by the Church has been oblivious, and at times even contemptuous, of what the thinker and the scholar can offer. It is better if the agenda for the scholar is set by the experience of the Church so that the ordinary Christian can humbly ask, 'What is the meaning of what I have experienced?'

Practical theology, if it is to escape from the grip of the fashionable, must have a Godward dimension. The triangle of theology and experience must always have at its apex the being of God. Indeed practical theology can legitimately go beyond the cerebral. As Karl Rahner said:

> Practical theology is that theological discipline which is concerned with the Church's self-actualization here and now ... It is neither a mere hotchpotch of practical con-

sequences or a collection of psychological, didactic, sociological rules of prudence, gained from the ordinary practice
of the care of souls. Practical theology should contain an
element of creativity and prophecy and be engaged in
critical reflection.[30]

Good theology is a theology which springs alive from the whole
'person-in-community'. It is not just intellectual contortions. On
the other hand it must not be the wrapping of theological
language around a religious experience (which is something
we shall see all too frequently in the history of renewals). 'You
shall love the Lord your God with all your heart . . . and soul
and mind' is as applicable to the doing of theology as to everything else.

THE SHAPE OF THE BOOK

The book is designed like a scientific study. Chapter 1 introduces the hypothesis which suggests that there is a 'normal'
progression in the history of a renewal. Chapter 2 gives a
brief introduction to the sociological ideas we shall be using.
Chapters 3 to 6 are four historical studies which test the hypothesis. They are deliberately chosen from different ages in the
Church's story – the New Testament, the medieval Cluniac
monastic revival, the Reformation and Counter Reformation,
and the American Awakenings. We shall use examples from
the modern renewal movements throughout. These are both
illustrative of the hypothesis and useful in teaching us about
other elements in the life of such movements.

Chapters 7 and 8 review the conclusions which have been
reached and tease out the lessons for the Church today, in its
local, denominational and worldwide manifestations. Finally,
Chapter 9 looks at the question behind the whole book. Is it
within the purposes of God that renewals change their nature?
Does the splendour always fade?

1 Hypothesis

ASSIMILATING NEW IDEAS

This book is built round an idea. It is left up to you, the reader, to decide whether or not the case is made.

New ideas go through certain stages. This has been recognised for a long time in scientific circles. If a new idea is introduced, whether it be Newton's law of gravity, or Wegener's tectonic plates, then there are certain patterns that are followed as it is absorbed by scientists. William Glen has studied the way in which the theory of continental drift and the theory of meteoric impact leading to the extinction of the dinosaurs were received by the scientific community.[1] He suggests that there are nine stages through which a new conception passes before it becomes part of mainstream thinking. The process may take many years because scientists can be as resistant to change as anyone else, and, as Peter Medawar remarked, 'many scientists unconsciously deplore the resolution of mysteries they have grown up with and therefore come to love'. These stages can be summarised as follows:

1. It all begins with a mystery – an unsolved problem that hangs like a question mark over some area of knowledge.
2. A new answer to the question is put forward, often by one person or a small group. It is seldom that a corporation or a large number of people reach an answer at the same time. Hence certain names attach themselves to certain discoveries: for example, Crick and Watson to the finding of the shape of the DNA molecule, Hubble to the discovery of distant galaxies, Harvey to the circulation of the blood.

The answer is not definitive – it is put forward as a hypothesis to be tested by others.

3. News of the hypothesis is circulated through scientific jour-
   nals, by word of mouth and sometimes by the wider media.

4. Because of the hostility which the hypothesis encounters,
   those who accept the hypothesis become the 'true believers'.
   These active proponents of the idea form an exclusive club
   who meet for conferences and write papers for each other.

5. The initial shock caused by the new idea gives way to a
   wary reaction as other experts in the field try to disprove
   the hypothesis. 'A new hypothesis is met with scepticism:
   by reasoned negative reactions from those who hold rival
   alternative views, and by knee-jerk negative reaction from
   those who oppose any radical new idea whatsoever.' It is
   at this point that some suggestions curl up and die or have
   such a large question mark put over them that they never
   thrive. NASA's claim to have found life forms in a meteorite
   discovered in Antarctica which was supposed to have come
   from Mars has just such a query hanging over it.

6. There follows the mobilisation of resources. Sometimes
   unexpected allies come from other disciplines. Tectonic
   plate theory, for instance, received massive encouragement
   from biologists and palaeontologists while geophysicists
   themselves were dismissive. A new debate, wider and less
   sceptical, begins.

7. The new theory collects around it a new terminology: jargon
   proliferates.

8. The silly season begins as the media get hold of the idea
   and then simplify, sensationalise and speculate.

9. Cooler heads prevail and the complexities of the theory
   become apparent. 'Both the original idea and its later manifestations are absorbed into a new mainstream.'

As we look at the list above it will be immediately apparent
that the acceptance of any renewal in the Church goes through
very similar stages. There is the original spark of renewal, there
are buckets of cold water which seek to extinguish it, there is

THE BASIC DIAGRAM

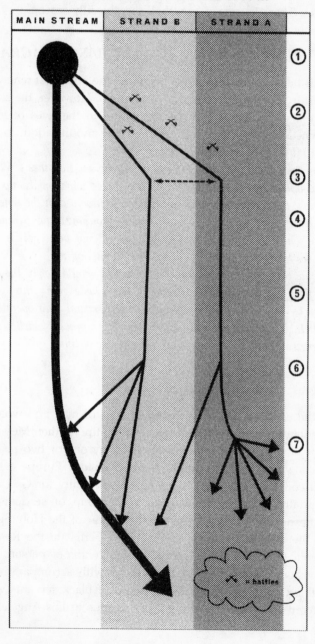

growth over years and then eventual absorption into the mainstream. There is even, as we shall see, the silly season.

THE SHAPE OF RENEWAL – THE BASIC DIAGRAM

In this book we shall examine primarily the impact of renewals in history on the life of the whole Church. However, the same study also applies with little adaptation to the lives of local churches. It can even apply, with greater modification, to the spiritual lives of individual Christians.

The basic diagram gives shape and form to the hypothesis. While this chapter will look primarily at the stages which make up the diagram, the significance of Strand A (those involved in the renewal who leave their churches to form a new grouping) and Strand B (those who remain in their churches) should not be forgotten. We shall see later in the book how vital this distinction is.

While the stages are set out in sequence, it should not be thought that they follow each other woodenly like people going through a turnstile. One can merge into another and several may operate in parallel. However, the overall pattern describes a process which nearly all renewals seem to undergo with the passage of time.

Stage 1: Renewal

On the edge of Jerusalem a small group of men and women experience something which sets them on fire for their Messiah. In the depths of the forests around Cluny one or two people have a vision of what might be. In war-torn Europe a tiny band commit themselves to being a community for God and eventually settle at Taizé. In 1967 a group of students at Duquesne University experience the power of the Holy Spirit and the charismatic renewal begins to permeate the Roman Catholic Church. Renewal usually begins with one person, like the vision Francis received in 1204, or with a comparatively small group of people, like the group of black servants who gathered at 214 North Bonnie Brae Avenue in Los Angeles in 1906.

Most renewals can be traced back to some such episode, whether it remains within a local church or spreads throughout the world. For those to whom it happens it is unmistakable, God-centred and unique. Afterwards they can never be the same people as before. There may well be new experiences of God but that first encounter can never be repeated. It feels like a personal 'conversion' or an 'infilling of the Holy Spirit' but it is much more than a stage in one person's spiritual journey: it is the beginning of something much wider, of significance for the Church and the world.

This is the age of discovery and experimentation. New ideas come tumbling out and are tried – to be either forgotten or adopted. In the American Revivals it was the establishing of the 'camp meeting'; in Cursillo the refining of the weekend conference. In medieval times it was the revolutionary idea that monks could wander from place to place rather than being immured in a monastery. Above all, the New Testament itself tells the story of how the Early Church learnt that God's purposes included even those who were not Jews: 'Then God has given even to the Gentiles the repentance that leads to life'.[2]

This is also the time for unselfconscious mission. Those in the renewal are so excited that they cannot but tell what they have experienced. From the disciples button-holing passers-by at Pentecost to the enthusiastic witness of someone who has been touched by God at a charismatic gathering, there is a longing to pass on the message which has captivated them. There is no need for campaigns or 'methods of evangelism' – it is spontaneous, natural and often effective, as the disciples found when thousands became believers. All things seem possible and it is only a matter of time before the world turns to Christ.

Stage 2: Conflict

'These men are filled with new wine': the mockery of Pentecost is inevitable. Any claim to a special visitation from God is bound to arouse mistrust, scepticism and rejection. Those who

the 'renewalists' live among have not had the same experience:
for them the world has not been turned upside down. Misunderstandings are bound to occur. The likelihood of this is
increased because those who are renewed have been 'surprised
by joy' and may show greater excitement than wisdom.

The deepest misunderstandings and the greatest rejection
often come from those within the Church who have not had
the same experience. The early New Church leaders in the
1960s, mainly from Brethren and Baptist chapels,[3] were subject
to outright hostility from those they had previously been
closest to. Several were excommunicated. Bishops and others
in positions of oversight are particularly prone to knee-jerk
reactions and may condemn a new movement out of hand.
There may well be excesses which give them some cause for
intervention and which widen any division: after all, any
complaints from those who are upset are likely to come
on to their desk. As Richard Lovelace says: 'successive eras of
church leaders have found it easy to immunise themselves
and their followers against awakening movements by applying
caricatures stressing the worst features of past revivals.'[4]

Stage 3: Networking

Conflict inevitably pushes those in the renewal closer together.
They try to find whether there are any others who have had
the same experience as themselves. They avidly read accounts
of similar happenings, and they meet together whenever possible. The Protestant leaders of the Reformation wrote letters to
each other, partly in order to give and receive support and
partly in order to talk about the new ideas which were bubbling
in their minds. The early charismatic movement was marked
by great conferences, each of them grander than the last. People
came from often hostile or uninterested churches and excitedly
found that they were not alone. Magazines proliferated, con-
taining testimonies of the work of God. Some people began to
try to work out what this experience meant theologically, but
in the early days the experience overrode the theology.

In some movements there are those who seek to advocate this networking from the beginning. Those who have been on a Cursillo are expected to enter the 'Fourth Day' when the Cursillistas commit themselves to meeting together regularly.

The 'in' language of the Cursillo movement with its talk of Ultreyas, and the 'mystagogy' and 'enlightenment' referred to by the catechumenate movement, illustrates another element of this phase. A new vocabulary develops, the nuances of which are known only to the initiated. They develop what Wayne Meeks calls 'the language of belonging',[5] a shorthand for those who are in the know. In some situations it becomes similar to the jargon of a secret society which is intended to obfuscate. This certainly irritates exceedingly those outside the movement who find its adherents incomprehensible.

To those within the renewal it begins to look as though they have the world at their feet. In medieval times the numbers of monasteries descended from a renewal such as Cluny multiplied a hundredfold. In modern times the networks get larger, the magazines glossier, the conferences bigger. A note of triumphalism begins to creep in as the enormous commitment and energy of those in the renewal is compared with the lacklustre quality of much Church life. Surely the whole Church must be changed by the exhilaration and drive of the new blood in her veins?

As the movement develops it is inevitable that certain individuals emerge into leadership positions. In relation to authority a renewal can have two kinds of beginning. The first kind is that which is dependent upon a guru, who is seen as the leader to be revered and obeyed. As time passes, the guru often loses some of his or her status as other leaders emerge. In a second model of renewal there is in the early stages a generally democratic pattern in which equality is predominant and decisions are made by consensus. However, it is inevitable that some people will come to be seen as more dynamic, or wiser, or more effective than others. Occasionally there is a deliberate attempt to usurp the place of the original leadership, particularly as the renewal passes to the next phase and issues of theology and practice become important.

Stage 4: Definition

By now the renewal has been in progress for some time. It finds that excited testimonies are not sufficient and it has to clarify its beliefs and practices more precisely.

This is a critical period in the life of any renewal. If the movement can do no more than define itself over against the mainstream of the theology of the Church, it is in peril. If it can do no more than draw up a manifesto of where it *disagrees* with others, it is likely to descend into division after division as the words of any statement of faith are haggled over and disputed. The American Awakenings defined themselves against 'liberalism' and against each other, and split and split again as a result. How much importance was the early Pentecostal movement to give to the phenomenon of speaking in tongues? Some saw it as essential while others regarded it as important but not normative. On this and other details the Pentecostal movement split into groupings which still remain. Mormonism and the Jehovah's Witnesses became more and more distant from the mainstream of Christianity as they defined themselves over against others. The Seventh Day Adventists have had an ongoing struggle as to whether they should be within the mainstream, albeit on the edge, or whether they should define the whole of their faith without reference to the rest of the Church.[6]

A sounder way forward is to seek to devise a theological definition which encompasses the whole of the Christian faith and seeks to integrate the new insights securely within the tradition of the whole Church. Otherwise there is an unhealthy emphasis on the differences and not sufficient acceptance of the areas of agreement. Luther, Calvin and the like carried out this work of theological integration at the time of the Reformation. Tom Smail and others did the same for the charismatic movement in the UK in the 1970s when there was a danger that it would take over a Pentecostal theology and forget what was old and tried and tested. He was able both to critique the emerging charismatic theology in the light of traditional theology and to show how the traditional could be infused by the insights of the charismatic.

Another factor may well intrude at this point. Often the original renewal was seen as a break for freedom. The old organisation, with its rules and restrictions, was left behind for the freedom of the gospel. Often in the new churches, old hierarchies were done away with and a more democratic pattern was established. As a renewal enters this stage when things are being defined more closely it is all too easy for the rules to be re-established and sometimes to become even more restrictive. At the Reformation the papacy and canon law were swept away, but it was not long before the new churches had even more rigid patterns than before.

This is particularly the case in moral matters. Freedom from the old can often be translated into a freedom from moral boundaries. It is all too common for this to be interpreted as licence, as Paul found when he may well have been echoing the words of a young Christian, 'Should we continue in sin in order that grace may abound?'.[7] The Church then moves swiftly to discipline the offender, and all too soon a framework of rules is established which can become a cage of iron. The freedom of the Reformation became the intrusion of the kirk into every detail of life for the people in Scotland in the sixteenth century, just as the freedom of the charismatic movement became the rigidity of 'discipling'.[8] The democratic ideals of the seventeenth-century Levellers and the idealistic pacifism of the Diggers soon faded under the constraints of the Puritans.[9]

The result of all this is institutionalisation. The movement gradually or quickly changes its spots. It becomes an organisation, with all the benefits and the disadvantages that ensue. Finance becomes more important. The evolution of an appropriate pattern of appointing and appraising leadership can no longer be avoided. There is more talk of buildings and personnel. Members begin to become tired as they realise that they are running a marathon, not a sprint. In the next chapter we shall look at what sociology can teach us about this very important phase.

Stage 5: Divergence

There now frequently occurs a significant phenomenon which is often unnoticed. The conflict and the networking makes the possibility of division real. Some people are thrown out of their churches, others withdraw from what they regard as a stony-faced refusal to face the truth of God. New groupings form with the characteristics of sects. There are all too many examples in Christian history, from the Montanists and the Donatists of the early centuries to the modern Pentecostal and New Church groupings.

Of equal significance, but often almost unremarked, there are those who do not leave the institutional church. They are touched by the renewal but struggle on in often unhelpful surroundings. They may gather in groups with others, for networking is an inevitable part of renewal, but they remain within their parent church. Their numbers may be very considerable. There were probably as many touched by Methodism who stayed within the Church of England as left it. The Counter Reformation, influenced by the strength of the Reformers' arguments, led to a reform movement within the Roman Catholic Church at the same time that the Protestant churches were being formed by those who seceded. Probably far more involved in the charismatic movement in Europe and America have stayed within the mainline churches than have left them.

Those who do not leave the institutional churches are inevitably caught in the cross-fire. On the one hand there is the uncomprehending institution within which they feel marginalised. On the other are those in the renewal who have seceded from their churches and regard those who remain loyal to the institution as half-hearted. Sometimes these who have separated will try to persuade those who remain in their churches to join them. 'Come thou with us and we will do thee good'[10] was an invitation given to many in the mainline churches by New Church members in the 1980s.

However, these 'halfway-house people' are of the greatest importance for the future of the movement. They are the communicators. They share the things of the renewal with the institutional church and they remain in contact with those who have split away. The divergence does not often become absolute. The Methodist Church continued to talk to evangelicals within the Church of England, and the leaders of the Counter Reformation were, cautiously, continuing to learn from the Protestant leaders.

The same divergence can happen with a local church. A group of people are touched by renewal, often through encountering it at some event outside their church such as a conference or presentation. They return and find that the fare provided by their church no longer satisfies. Some depart and either form their own church or join another which is more to their liking. Others, though still disenchanted with their church, remain and seek to change the church from within – often throwing themselves into the life of the church with great energy. Sometimes, however, they form a small group on the edge of the church and have little to do with the rest of the congregation.

As in the diagram, for ease of reference in this book we shall call these groupings as follows:

> Strand A – those who leave their churches and form new groupings
> Strand B – those who remain in their churches
> Mainstream – those in the churches who are largely unaffected by the renewal

Stage 6: Outside Communication

Years, even centuries, have passed. The renewal has been long established. In the life of a local church all the upset when it went Anglo-catholic or charismatic is long past. It is now part of the tradition. Those who have departed into Strand A may now be into their second generation; their new leaders will have been brought up in that church and know no other. Those churches which were formed as a result of the division after the renewal have now settled down – the early fires have died down to not much more than a gentle smouldering. The movements which were to overcome the world have become denominations.

And communication now begins to take place with the Church outside. For those who split from their parent churches there had been a tendency in the early days to think of other Christians either as only semi-Christians or even to exclude them from the Kingdom altogether. Their churches were dismissed as hopelessly corrupt and weak. Now meeting takes place across the old divides. Whether at some ecumenical gathering that previously would have been shunned with a shudder or on a mission, they meet others who call themselves Christians. They are surprised: they find they are talking to people whose love of God in Christ is as rich as their own, whose prayers are real and whose lives reflect their faith. They expect antagonism and find friendliness. Relationships begin.

For those who have remained within their previous church structures communication with the mainstream is easier. They may well find that initial suspicions begin to die down and the message they bring is listened to. The assumption that they are denominational pariahs begins to be shown to be wrong. Their theology is regarded respectfully[11] and their experiences of God are listened to without mockery. They find themselves increasingly accepted as a normal part of the life of the church. There may even be encouraging voices from on high, as the Catholic charismatics found in papal statements in the 1970s and 1980s, and as the followers of the Counter Reformation found ten generations earlier, and indeed as St Francis found ten generations before that.

Stage 7: Consequences

The stage is set for the denouement. There are three possible scenarios:

Stage 7a: Fragmentation

Churches which have formed as a result of splitting from their parent body after a renewal are always in a delicate condition. If they have chosen the wrong path in each of the previous stages they are in grave danger. It is often perceived as an identity crisis. They ask, 'Who are we?'; 'What makes us different?'.

If they have defined themselves against the rest of the Christian Church without seeing how their insights fit into the whole of Christian doctrine they will end up arguing about words and practices. Is a cup of tea a dangerous stimulant? Is their Statement of Faith to include X and exclude Y? Because there is no outside authority they are particularly susceptible to personality clashes among the leadership. Personal quarrels are dressed up as theological disagreements, and real theological differences become personalised. The result is a further split. Nor does it end there. The resulting pieces of that split are themselves liable to divide again. In the end the whole fragments into nothingness. The river ends as a multitude of trickles in the sand and then dries up altogether. For example, in 1732 the Seceders left the General Assembly of the Church of Scotland. They soon split into Burghers and Anti-burghers, Auld Lichts and New Lichts, Lifters and Anti-lifters, in a succession of smaller and smaller units until the movement ultimately ran into nothingness.

Stage 7b: Denomination or religion

If the new churches spawned by the renewal movement have made their new insights part of the whole Christian tradition, and if they have begun to communicate with others and recognise them as Christians, then they will become yet another denomination in the Christian firmament. They will develop the inevitable characteristics of a denomination. Some years ago I met a New Church leader who vehemently denied that he led a denomination. I pointed out that they now had budgets and headquarters, organisations and annual conferences. He fell silent.

If the renewal is deep and there is a profound division with the mainline faith, or if the renewal sees itself as so free of the past that it makes up its own faith, then a new religion can be born. Thus the Christian faith grew out of its Jewish matrix, and many new faiths have been produced from Hindu, Christian or Buddhist roots.

Stage 7c: Assimilation

For those who have stayed within their church, assimilation is both a goal and a danger. The danger is that they lose the surge of prayer, thinking and action which spurred them upwards in the early days and they relapse into mediocrity. Their renewal days of long ago excite merely a pleasant nostalgia or a dispiriting memory of what might have been. We shall see how easily the medieval monasteries became as distant from the idealism of their founders as all the rest. The American revivals tried to resist the ordinariness of church life but failed. Many who have had a 'charismatic experience' look back on it wistfully. We may even find that this process has an inevitability about it that we shall need to come to terms with.

However, something else may be going on which is less easy to distinguish but much more important. As the mainstream of the home denomination begins to soften the edges of the renewal, so the renewal begins to influence the whole denomination. The Roman Catholic Church was profoundly affected by the Counter Reformation; the American Awakenings touch the American churches to this day. The same has been true in the charismatic movement, as an official report to the Church of England on the movement stated:

> The 'behavioural gap' has narrowed *from the non-charismatic side* ... there are many non-charismatic parishes feeling

their way to a greater openness, a deeper experience of
the Spirit, an 'every member ministry' and other features
characteristic of the movement.[12]

Thus assimilation should sometimes be regarded, not as something to be regretted, but as something to be deeply desired
and prayed for as the direction of the whole church is changed.
The renewal becomes the rudder for the whole ship.

If new denominations have formed as a result of Strand A
then the process of assimilation will be delayed. Communication is more difficult because each denomination develops in
time a life of its own. While individual Christians can meet
gladly, denominational structures have to be taken into account
and they are notoriously impervious to ecumenical imperatives.
The result is that while assimilation may take place as ideas
cross from one denomination to another, the osmosis is much
more difficult and easily prevented by extraneous matters. Thus
the dialogue between the churches of the Reformation and the
Roman Catholic Church are complicated by the need for official
statements and such non-theological matters as different
authority structures and social backgrounds.

AN ALTERNATIVE MODEL

The model described above is the one we shall be using in this
book. However, there is another which is more personal and
less organisational. It may help to explain some of the human
reactions in a renewal which can be at least as important as the
spiritual impetus or the managerial requirements. It is too easy
to see the progress of a renewal only in terms of theological
ideas and organisational developments: there are human beings
involved too, with all their emotions and irrationalities. Pride,
ambition and envy as well as idealism, friendship and
excitement all have their part to play.

As this is a matter of relationships it is best approached
through the use of story, though the appropriate stages in the
diagram are indicated from time to time.

Once upon a time Peter and Sheila lived in a medium-sized house in the middle of suburbia. They were a rather medium sort of people, with ordinary views on contemporary issues; they had an ordinary income and an ordinary house. They were pretty average and unexciting sort of people but loving and kind to their two children. Jennifer was sixteen at the time this story starts – she thought her own thoughts and had began to grow away from her parents during her adolescence. Michael was a couple of years older, doing well at school and looking forward to university and getting a job.

Both the children went to the local comprehensive, and it was there that one day they met a friend, Bob, who was going on a protest rally against a road which was being carved through the countryside nearby. Both Jennifer and Michael had been mildly interested in ecological matters for some time and Jennifer had flirted with vegetarianism for a short while until the smell of fish and chips had tempted her one evening and she had fallen. They were persuaded by Bob to go with him to a meeting about the road.

Stage 1. *They had never encountered anything like it before. The room was packed with young people. Their own thoroughly conventional clothes stood out among the nose studs, the boots and the leathers. But the meeting was electric – there was no speaker, but lots of people spoke about the road and what they could do to stop it. Michael and Jennifer were bemused, thrilled and challenged. They talked excitedly about it on the way home and decided that they would join the protest which was beginning soon. When they got home they poured out the story to their parents.*

Stage 2. *Peter's reaction came first – he was appalled. He had never done anything out of the ordinary all his life and the thought of his children joining a lot of long-haired, drug-taking layabouts filled him with horror. Indeed the notion of his children doing something altruistic, guided by a desire to help others, was something he could not get his head round. Sheila was in her own way equally worried, only she worried about the dangers they would face, the university course that might slip away, and how they were going to do their washing. There was a row, which began with stiff politeness and ended with shouts and insults and slammed doors.*

Stage 3. *In the weeks before the protest began the atmosphere hardened. Jennifer began to dye her hair and Michael bought a studded jacket, which he wore rather self-consciously. They began to read books which seemed to Peter to be subversive of all ordered society. Far more influential, though unknown to Peter and Sheila, was the Internet, through which protesters from around the world spoke to each other and published details of events and sit-ins. Sitting in front of their computer screen they felt they were part of a great revolt of youth against the mechanised, commercialised world they had come to despise.*

Peter voiced his concern by starting to lay the law down as to when they could come and go. Sheila wept silently. Unspoken at the back of their minds was what the neighbours thought of their rebellious children: they confided only in their closest friends who told them it was only a phase, saying 'they'll soon get over it'. The youngsters became more and more determined. Secretly they longed for a rational discussion but that seemed impossible and soon they were as entrenched as their parents as they continued to go to the planning meetings.

Stage 4. *Michael and Jennifer felt part of a great crusade for what was right against the powers of darkness – the developers and the car manufacturers would cover Mother Earth with concrete. Pride, stubbornness, and misunderstanding were building a higher and higher wall. Jennifer and Michael felt they were engaged in something more exciting and more worthwhile than anything they had ever done before and yet they could not get through to their parents. If their schoolwork suffered that was as nothing compared with the great things they were doing. What were exam results compared with saving the planet?*

Stage 5. *Things came to a head one evening when Peter complained bitterly about how they were wasting all the money he had spent on their education. Michael stormed out of the house, slamming the door behind him. Jennifer rushed upstairs in tears. Michael stayed the night with one of his new friends in a squat and the next day came to collect his things. Apart from a postcard saying that he was all right he made no contact with his parents for months and Sheila* *was worried out of her mind. Jennifer still saw him at the meetings, but he had changed: he wanted her to join him – to be completely committed to the cause. She was torn between the comfort of her own home and the primitive conditions of the squat, between loyalty to her brother and her genuine love for her parents.*

The protest itself brought together people from Europe and the Americas as well as those from the UK. The protesters split into three groups. The tunnellers were regarded as the 'hard' men and women, much admired by the rest. Some climbed trees while others formed a mobile flying picket, getting in the way of the contractor's lorries and lying down in front of the police to hamper them getting at the others. Michael and Jennifer were in this last group. At first it was exciting, rushing from place to place trying to forestall and outwit the 'enemy'. The police were initially amiable, but later frustrated and eventually heavy-handed. Both Michael and Jennifer were arrested and bound over to keep the peace.

But for both of them the moments which mattered were the times round the campfires in the evening when ideas flew across the flames and they found their own minds becoming formed by the anarchists and the radicals they met. For Michael in particular it all made sense: if there was no property, there would be no possessions and if there were no possessions no one would want to take anything from anyone, and then there would be no war, no quarrels and no crime. In her heart Jennifer was not so sure but she was swept along with the arguments.

Stage 6. *After six weeks it was over. The police moved in in force, the contractors sawed down the trees and the tunnels were emptied. During all this time the two had had no communication with their parents, and all Sheila and Peter learnt was from the reports in the Daily Telegraph. Peter was appalled, while Sheila found herself secretly rather proud of them for having the strength to stand up for themselves, though she never admitted it to a soul. Even she began to have doubts when her daughter came home. Jennifer was defiant, brash, rude and noisy. There were times when she showed a milder side to her mother but with her father it was argument after argument.*

Michael never contacted them except for a Christmas card and a small present for his mother's birthday – never one for his father. Through Jennifer they heard that he was living with friends, going to protests, living hand to mouth. Though Jennifer never said as much, they suspected he was on drugs and worried themselves sick with the thought that Jennifer might be on them as well. Often she came back in the early hours and twice she disappeared for several days together with hardly a word of explanation.

Stage 7. This is a post-modern story so you will have to make up your own ending from the three scenarios below.

(a)   It could end in tears. Michael might be killed in his squat by violence or an overdose, and Jennifer might squander her life in abortions, poverty and single parenthood in a series of fleeting relationships with men.

(b)   Alternatively, this wing of the ecological movement might begin to find that direct confrontations were less productive than political action. With their intelligence, Michael and Jennifer could find themselves as potential leaders of this emerging force in society.

(c)   Another option might be that the established political parties found there was something in the 'green' outlook which struck a chord with the public and decided to do more than fidget with these issues. Cars were severely restricted, roads were built only when absolutely necessary, global warming was accepted as a real threat (a view accelerated when the underground in London was flooded by the rising North Sea bursting the Greenwich barrage). A landmark was reached when a stretch of the M6 was taken up and returned to agriculture. Michael ended as a civil servant in the Department of Ecology and Jennifer took her degree in forestry and went to plant trees in Brazil.

Two final points should be made. This is not an improbable story. Something like it has happened to many families. Does this suggest that the progress of a renewal is nothing to do with 'spiritual decline' or 'the work of the devil' but is a natural

human process which we should expect? Ought we even to
expect and control it?

Secondly, you made your own choice about which of the
three scenarios was the most likely outcome. Does this mean
that we have a degree of control over the way in which renewal
impacts on the whole Church?

2 *Sociology and All That*

'Ask sociologists any question and our response is likely to be a contemplative silence, a scholarly scowl, and finally, a long list of methodological conundrums leading to that ultimate conclusion, "It all depends".[1] That wry comment from Jay Demerath shows, first, that sociologists have a sense of humour, and second, that their conclusions are not infallible. Nevertheless when discussing renewals it is important to take a sociological viewpoint from time to time. This chapter, therefore, will look at some of the issues raised by sociologists and how they apply to Christian renewals and (to a lesser extent) to New Religious Movements[2] and to other faiths.

One of the founding fathers of modern sociology was the Frenchman Emile Durkheim (1858–1917). He described religion as 'a social product . . . with a unified system of beliefs and practices which unite into one single moral community all those who adhere to them'. Subsequently 'religion' has been regarded as a 'social product' and studied academically like any other field of human activity.

Christians have been understandably wary of a sociological approach. It is inevitably this-worldly, matter-of-fact and seems to devalue the spiritual in the quest for all-too-human explanations. As Bryan Wilson says, sociology is 'an onslaught against the theological, and against the supernatural entities (beings, laws, events, places, and actions) which religion projected as of real determining importance'. In other words, God gets left out.

However, any study of human behaviour is valuable to those who have faith in the God 'who knows your hearts'.[3] Certainly

no study of renewals can get far without recognising all the
human factors which are at work in them. In renewals we can
find idealism and manipulation, foolishness and wisdom, great
commitment and dilettantism. Further, sociologists have made
comments on renewals and their progress which are interesting:
we must make up our own minds as to how far their theories
correspond with reality.

There are certain caveats which have to be made at the
beginning.

1. Sociologists have been much more concerned with those
   who are in 'sects' – Strand A in our diagram – than with
   those who have remained in the mainstream churches –
   Strand B. They have therefore tended to study what may
   well be atypical and extreme.
2. Few sociologists are members of the groups they are de-
   scribing. They therefore have an outsider's point of view,
   and because of this may miss the main motivations and
   dynamics of the body they are investigating.
3. Human beings are pattern-making creatures and sociologists are no exception. They can therefore try to make a
   theory they have produced cover all situations. Inevitably,
   therefore, there are exceptions which do not fit the theory
   and these may be either ignored or forced to conform. For
   example, we shall come across the suggestion that renewals
   only happen at times of social disturbance: is this a general
   law or are there so many exceptions that the 'law' is no law
   at all?
4. Most sociologists we read tend to live within a Western
   context – and hence one deeply influenced by the Christian
   faith. Therefore the 'religion' they have in mind is likely
   to be Christianity. This can be significant. For example,
   Durkheim and others hold that all religions divide the
   world into the sacred and the profane. In reality, by no
   means all do. Indeed, is it true of Christianity?
5. Most sociologists work within an academic environment.
   There is therefore a tendency to assume that the more

rational a religion is and the more efficient its organisation, the more it will prosper. But it may well be that it is precisely the irrational elements which are more significant. Is it our reaction to what Rudolf Otto called the 'mysterium tremendum et fascinosum' of the Holy which is the true motivation of a religion?

6. Above all, from the Christian standpoint, the sociologist seeks objectivity and tries to be free of judgemental attitudes. Whether looking at a Japanese sect which seeks to kill non-members or the most benign of Christian activists for peace, no moral distinctions are drawn by most sociologists. Not all would agree with this. For example, Sorokin, who was described as a 'conservative libertarian and Christian anarchist',[4] argued that since sociologists were themselves products of their environment they inevitably imbibed many of its value judgements and hence were never unbiased observers. It was better that this was recognised rather than disguised under a cloak of supposed impartiality. He instances the concept of time. This is culturally as well as scientifically conditioned. Different communities, depending on their custom, judge time differently: some use the sun, others the stars or the passage of the seasons. It is only when separate communities seek to communicate that the need for common yardsticks becomes necessary. Early last century the time in each town in the UK varied a little as each gauged the time from the position of the sun at their particular point of longitude. For example, Bristol set its clocks ten minutes later than London. It was the coming of the railways which forced a common time on the nation, so that, for instance, trains leaving at 9.15 a.m. left at the same time across the UK. It was called 'railway time' and only slowly became universal.[5]

To be fair to the sociologists, many now realise the false results they may produce by not getting under the skin of those they are trying to understand. Many now practise 'participant observation', by which the observer becomes to some degree part of the community he or she is studying. First applied to the study of native peoples, it is now seen as essential for the study of any religious, political or ethnic group. Sociologists 'should attempt to understand people's behaviour from the perspective of the latter's own cultural and religious norms and values'.[6]

BELIEF, FAITH AND BELONGING

Before going further we have to examine more deeply the Western bias of sociology. Do sociologists, because of the Western emphasis on the individual, pay too much attention to what people believe? Further, do credal statements define a religion? These are significant in the Christian faith but are they as important as we think? Indeed, many would say that Christianity is based on commitment to a person rather than belief in a creed. Is it appropriate to ask of anyone as a first question, 'What do you believe?'. Many sociologists and many Christians do not realise how unusual this is, nor do we always understand that other factors are often more important to any individual.

In some societies, what someone believes is almost irrelevant. In such cases the religious practices of the community are far more important than what any individual in that community thinks. Thus it is entirely possible to be a Jew and not believe in God. Kibbutzim who marry atheists nearly always ask that their partners should become Jews: they need to join the community.[7]

Malcolm Ruel set out four 'shadow fallacies' which Christians can easily slip into:

(a) that belief is as central to other religions as it is to Christianity;

(b) 'that the belief of a person or of a people forms the ground of his or her behaviour';

(c) 'that belief is fundamentally an interior state, a psychological condition';

(d)   that in Christianity allegiance to a belief is more important than knowledge of the content of that belief.[8]

It is important to be aware of this in our study of renewals. The significance of the community cannot be divorced from the belief of the individual. As we shall see in our study of New Religious Movements, a dominant community can inculcate in its members the most bizarre beliefs. The influence of the fellowship of believers – for good or ill – cannot be under-played. The Nürnberg rallies were chilling reminders of the shadow side of ideology, for they were expressions both of intellectual assent and of faith.

We also need to understand that intellectual assent to a faith can be vastly different from 'faith', defined in terms of volitional motivation. In human terms faith is akin to 'love'. The New Testament defines it in those terms: the second half of John chapter 14 is an exploration by Christ of what it means for a disciple to 'love me'. C. S. Lewis, in his classic work *The Four Loves* shows how the different patterns of love interweave and reinforce each other. For him faith has elements of affection, friendship, 'eros' and charity – and also of that love given from outside 'a supernatural Appreciative Love towards Himself'.[9]

In this book we shall need to have at the back of our mind an awareness of the different kinds of 'faith'. Faith can be seen as:. (a) assent to a creed, (b) commitment to a person or a movement, and (c) belonging to a certain group of people. Different forms of renewal will have different combinations of these forms of faith.

ENTHUSIASM

While faith is one of the motivations we shall encounter, what gives faith its emotional driving force is enthusiasm. Without it, faith can be a flaccid thing. Most renewals, almost by de-finition, are enthusiastic movements. They have a passion about them which can be alarming for onlookers and which seems at times to override common sense. At the same time their intensity attracts – here are people who really believe. In his study of religious experience in Zulu Zionist churches in South Africa, Jim Kiernan describes one of their services as 'inspirational and random': 'Throughout the meeting there is a release and expenditure of tremendous energy so that at the end participants are drained and completely spent.'[10]

Psychologists who examined a British black Pentecostal congregation with a similar style of worship had to admit that they were remarkably well-balanced people. Such apparent excess does not appear to harm the participants any more than raucous involvement in a football match harms those taking part. Indeed it may be emotionally liberating: certainly it is experienced as spiritually uplifting.

'Enthusiasm' has had a mixed career. Originally it meant 'being possessed by a god', but in a reaction to the excesses of the English Civil War at the end of the seventeenth century it became a negative word denoting religious fanaticism and outlandish behaviour. Indeed it was 'a code word for the excesses of spurious revival since the days of the Reformation'.[11] This was true of the Puritan Richard Baxter as well as those who were imbued with the cool theism of the eighteenth century. In his Dictionary, Samuel Johnson defined it as 'a vain confidence of Divine favour or communication'. Early Methodism was described as enthusiastic, and this was not intended as a compliment.[12] In 1868 Disraeli advised Queen Victoria against appointing Bishop Tait to Canterbury, with the delicious words: 'There is in his idiosyncrasy a strange fund of enthusiasm, a quality which ought never to be possessed by an Archbishop of Canterbury'.

However, while the word was at first confined to religion, it later became used for any interest pursued with zest, whether it be bee-keeping or stamp collecting. In the last century or so 'enthusiasm' has come to be regarded as a positive word opposed to such words as 'prosaic', 'uncreative', 'dull'.

Inevitably, since enthusiasm describes a human drive with a strong emotional content, enthusiasts speak often of *experience*. This presents problems, for most experiences are capable of more than one interpretation: as Dr Johnson was inferring, a prophetic word may to the enthusiast be the voice of God while to an onlooker it may seem entirely human in origin. As Locke pointed out, speaking in the late seventeenth century, and doubtless mindful of the excesses of the Civil War period when many self-professed prophets sought to be heard:

> The question then here is: how do I know that God is the revealer of this to me, that the impression is made on my mind by his Holy Spirit, and that therefore I ought to obey it? If I know not this, how great so ever the assurance is that I am possessed with, it is groundless, whatever light [i.e. spiritual perception] I pretend to, it is but enthusiasm.

The root question is: 'What criterion do we use to judge a statement or an experience?' That is one of those foundational philosophical questions of far wider importance than the issues surrounding renewal. Descartes reduced it to the individual – 'I think, therefore I exist' – and tried to build an inverted pyramid of philosophy on that rather rickety point. The instability of the Cartesian approach can be seen by the very different conclusions which can be drawn from other starting points. Many people in less individualistic or less secular environments might start with 'God is, therefore I exist' or '*we* think, therefore *we* exist'. Indeed we may agree with Hume in his critique of Descartes that there can be no *guaranteed* foundation for human philosophy and that there is no fulcrum round which we can build a rational system of thought.

It is impossible to go into the philosophical issues here but the subject is of fundamental importance in discussing renewal movements, because for many people involved in them *experience* is of at least equal value to theological precision.[13] It can therefore be difficult from outside to understand their motivations and those personally involved are not always able to 'give a reason for the hope that is in them'. As a result they may be categorised as 'simplistic', 'over-emotional', 'experience-orientated' or 'extreme'.

However the cool look from outside can be helpful. We shall

find that sometimes secular commentators studying renewal movements, and trying to take an objective view, can be more perceptive than Christians who have a theological framework against which they are measuring a movement. This is particularly true when looking at New Religious Movements, especially those connected with New Age thinking.

There is another element which has to be taken into account in evaluating a renewal movement's credentials and this is the fact that it is not always possible to be precise. People tend to ask, 'Is this true' and, like too many television interviewers, expect 'Yes' or 'No' as an answer. Sometimes you have to say, 'It is partly true, partly false'. There is the divine mixed with the all-too-human. As Tom Smail said of the prophecies in the current charismatic movement, 'The best prophecies only have a third from God, but what a third'.[14]

However, sociologists have come to recognise an important element in the emotional level of enthusiasm within a movement. It is not a steady decline from an initial high point. It can be rekindled. One of the most common ways in which this happens is when the members of a group enter a new and challenging environment. In the United States this has often been seen in immigrant churches. Before the church members entered their new country their church-going was often spasmodic at best. But when they entered a strange and potentially hostile new world their church was their only point of reference. It possessed a social structure in which they felt at home, it often retained the language, food and styles of worship of their home country. In 1916, for instance, 49 per cent of Roman Catholics in the US worshipped in a language which was not English.[15] The boundary between the church and its context, which had been low in the immigrants' home countries, suddenly increased and they sought refuge in the church's familiarity. The same phenomenon has often been remarked on when members of a faith go overseas, and it is particularly true of those members of other faiths who have entered Britain in recent years.

This element is of importance in local church situations,

where a move to a more threatening environment can often lead to greater commitment. This might involve a church plant in a difficult environment, an ex-patriot community overseas or even outright persecution.

DEFINITIONS

There are several words which need to be more precisely defined before we can use them freely and appropriately.

Sect

As already mentioned in the Introduction, this is a word used in sociology without the negative overtones of normal speech. It is usually contrasted with the word 'church'. Thus it has been defined as: 'a revolutionary movement which sets against the Church a point of view in which the Church has become conservative and fixed'.

Bryan Wilson defines the characteristic structure of a sect as having:

- a clearly defined community;
- a coherent structure of value;
- an element of protest conditioned by the economic, social, ideological and religious circumstances prevailing at the time of its emergence and development.

Obviously such descriptions are far wider than the purely religious and could cover such groups as Freemasons, some political parties and even ecological groups such as Greenpeace. He goes on to describe a religious sect as: 'an all-embracing, divinely prescribed society'.[16]

A sect has a clear boundary. Because of this there is a considerable emphasis on initiation into membership. The sect is entered by some semi-contractual arrangement by which the entrant agrees to certain requirements and the sect pledges its protection and fellowship. Some sociologists describe such an entity as a 'bounded set' and it is by no means confined to religious organisations.

This use of the word 'sect' means, of course, that a number of bodies which are normally called 'churches' are, in sociological terms, 'sects'. Those churches, mainly in the Reformed tradition, which lay a great stress on membership are, sociologically speaking, sects. Once again we need to notice that this is not used pejoratively. We should also notice that many bodies which are strongly exclusive and clearly sects in sociological terms, call themselves 'church' – like the Church of Scientology.

The sociological use of the word has its advantages and we shall use it in this sense in this chapter. In terms of our basic diagram, the breakaway groups designated as Stream A are, sociologically speaking, sects.

Church

Sociologists use the word 'church' in a different way from the one we are used to. To them the word describes the stable and unchanging organisation from which the sect emerges.[17] It also has a use which is wider than the merely religious. Thus it can refer to the mainstream Christian churches, but it also encompasses the main bodies from which have emerged such varied groups as the Trotskyites, the Animal Liberation Movement and the British Social Democrats of the 1980s.

Sociologists would say that a church is an 'open set'. There is much less emphasis on boundaries, and it is not always easy to say who are members and who are not. Obviously in our basic diagram, the mainstream and Strand B are 'church' in sociological terms.

Charisma

This word was used by Weber to describe a particular characteristic. He defines it as 'a certain quality of an individual personality by which he or she is set apart from ordinary people and treated as a leader'. It may be the military charisma of a 'born leader'. It may be the political charisma of someone for whom people cast their vote. It may be religious charisma, demonstrated by prophecy or magic (it is here that the link with the modern Christian use of the word 'charismatic' is closest). Indeed many who are clearly seen to possess charisma will have elements from all three types – leadership potential, the ability to inspire allegiance and acknowledged as having special powers.

Normally a charismatic leader is unique. However some movements try to establish a succession of such leaders. In the political field it can be seen in the institution of monarchy or the hereditary peerage. In religion the institutions of the papacy and the Dalai Lama seek the same sort of immortality. In the person of the Japanese Emperor, until very recently, political and religious charisma were fused. Where there is such a continuation of charisma down the generations there is usually some form of 'handing on' ceremony. This can be a coronation, a consecration or an enthronement, at which the handing on of the old charisma to the new person is emphasised. When this happens charisma can turn head over heels, becoming not a force for change and new thinking but for traditionalism and the status quo. The radical becomes conservative. As Weber says:

> We find that peculiar transformation of charisma into an institution: permanent structures and traditions replace the belief in the revelation and heroism of charismatic personalities, charisma becomes part of an established social structure.[18]

Weber also describes the way in which a charismatic leader gathers around himself or herself a 'staff'. These are not officials or people particularly trained for their roles, but those whom the leader gathers for personal support and friendship and for the executing of his or her ideas. They are generally people who are particularly committed to the ideas of the leader and prepared to accept their vision and make it happen. They may well have a function in protecting the leader from intrusion if the demands of people outside become excessive, in which case they are seen as 'gatekeepers' who allow or forbid access. They may well be less than popular with others within the movement because they are perceived both as acting as a defensive shield around the leader and also as having privileged familiarity. It is noticeable that most presidents and prime ministers gather such a group around them which is quite distinct from the official cabinet. In a church a similar process often operates, as the minister gathers together a group of people which is different from the offical church committee.[19]

Sociologists point out that, once the founder of the movement has passed from the scene, the 'staff' become the 'holders of the vision', determined that the memory and the ideas of the founder should not be sullied or changed. It is often from among the 'staff' that the next leader arises.

The application of this to the New Testament is obvious and we shall look at it in the next chapter. This also explains why Judas Iscariot is particularly execrated – he was 'staff', and therefore owed a particular loyalty to the leader he should have revered and supported. He became the *paradidous* – 'the one who handed over', who betrayed not only a person but also the whole tradition entrusted to him.

(When considering definitions it is interesting to notice that there is no special sociological nomenclature to describe Stream B, the middle line of our diagram – those affected by the renewal but who do not leave to join a sect and stay within the church. When looking at the sociological insights we need to bear in mind that this is a picture of extremes.)

THE ROUTINISATION OF CHARISMA

The process of routinisation has been described by many.[20] David Bosch says:

> Either a movement disintegrates or it becomes an institution – this is simply a sociological law. Every religious

group that started out as a movement and managed to
survive, did so because it was gradually institutionalised:
the Waldensians, the Moravians, the Quakers, the
Pentecostals . . .

The process was described fully by Weber in 1946, though
Niebuhr and others had described it in less detail earlier.[21] It is
the way in which a sect becomes a church. Never does a church
turn into a sect.[22] Typically in its early days a Moses figure
leads a group away from the idle fleshpots and slavery of a
church which has become effete and disobedient to God. The
pattern of our diagram begins to take shape – the battles, the
networking, the beginnings of definition – ('What makes us so
special?'). But the passage of time and, often, the departure of
the original leaders from the scene, means that the sect settles
down to a routine. As Weber says: 'When the tide that lifted a
charismatically led group out of everyday life flows back into
the channels of workaday routines, at least the pure form of
charismatic denomination will wane and turn into an institution.'[23]

Generally this process, whether in a national or an international movement, is seen as retrograde. Spiritual power is
thought to decrease, the excitement level becomes less frenetic,
disappointment with the intractability and sinfulness of the
world is increasingly voiced. Is this an appropriate response to
institutionalisation? The process seems to be almost inevitable.
Is it sensible to resist it? James Burchaell says:

> Institutionalisation is a stabilised consensual conversion of
> relationships into roles and then into custom, duty and
> office. It need not happen – indeed, it does not happen –
> by anyone's conscious effort. It is imposed by the sheer
> logic of group life and group development, and only in
> retrospect does it become obvious.[24]

While there are nuances to this process, which Weber's critics
have drawn attention to,[25] the pattern is too common to be
rejected. It seems to be the normal process by which a move-

ment matures. Are we right to deplore it, bemoan it and fight against it or should we seek to manage the process appropriately? In other words, should we accept its inevitability calmly as a natural part of being human?

There are some interesting elements which have been discerned in this process and we will look briefly at some of them here.

Boundaries

Any organisation has to have a boundary if it is to survive. A nation needs to know whom it can tax, a club has to have a list of its subscribers, a church wants to have some idea of those who belong.

A boundary means that inevitably there are those who are outside it. Even those who wish to be all-inclusive find that there are some who do not fit. A Christian universalist who wishes all to be Christian even if they do not know it, finds that there are many of other faiths and none who do not wish to be so embraced. A Jew or a Hindu or a Muslim is far too proud of their religion to wish to be patronised.

The relation between a sect and those outside is crucial. If the outside is perceived as hostile then the sect becomes defensive and increasingly isolated. In the early days of a sect its members regard the church they have recently left as the main source of animosity. They see the people there, even those they had once counted as their friends, as unspiritual and conservative because they too did not leave. A local church encounters this when a group leaves: relationships sour and may even be broken entirely. Resonances of it can be found in the New Testament in the way some Gentile Christians viewed those Jews who allied their Christianity with their Jewish faith.

The attitude of the Church may well help to build the boundaries higher. Church members see the formation of the sect as a judgement upon themselves or their Church by those who break away (as indeed it often is). They lose members, break long friendships. The early Methodists were excluded from the

Church of England, Edward Irving from the Church of Scotland, and the early New Church leaders like Campbell McAlpine and Arthur Wallis from their Brethren and Baptist churches. The synagogues excluded Christians officially by the *birkath ha-minim*.[26] There may well be social and ethnic as well as theological factors also at work. The early Pentecostal Church found it difficult to maintain its early tolerance of members who were poor and black, particularly when they were in positions of leadership like James Seymour.[27]

Where members of the sect feel that there is persecution, not just from the church from which they sprang, but also from the society in which they live, then the sense of isolation can become profound. Whether they are right in this perception or not is immaterial: their boundary is strengthened and the world outside becomes an unfamiliar place. Indeed paranoia can become apparent and everything, however innocent, is drawn into a world view which sees all things outside the sect as imbued with evil. Satan's hand is suspected in all that happens.

Normally this sense of isolation lessens with time. However if there are periodic actions which seem to reinforce the sense of persecution then the boundaries remain formidably high. Thus Steve Bruce shows how terrorist atrocities repeated down the years reinforce the world view of many Ulster Protestants. When this is allied with the culture of Ian Paisley's Free Presbyterian Church, it forms a mindset intensely suspicious of change.[28]

It is often trite to say that 'time is the great healer'. In the progress of renewals this may be so if reinforcement of tensions does not occur. The local parish church learns to pray with the New Church which was founded by its ex-members. The scars of the Reformation are lessened by ecumenism. It becomes increasingly difficult to hold to the belief that the normal world in which you earn a living and go shopping is totally under the domain of Satan. The boundaries begin to become lower.

Successful sect movements develop strong internal pressures to lower their tension with the surrounding culture.

These pressures come from having an increasingly affluent membership and from a 'professionalised' clergy... together they begin to lift restrictions on behaviour and to soften doctrines... a process known as sect transformation or secularisation.[29]

The process described as *legitimation* by sociologists has begun. As the boundaries become lower there is an attempt to construct a modus vivendi with society. Particularly as the second or third generation of new members join the organisation, legitimation becomes important if a sect is to survive.

There are several different ways in which this process can be seen, the first two of which are mentioned in the quotation above.

1. *The membership becomes increasingly affluent.*
    The sect's members, because of the ethical demands of their faith, are honest and hardworking. They get better jobs – and with it a desire for some of the trappings of belonging to a respectable organisation. They are no longer content with the tin tabernacle in which they found God: they want a 'proper' church and now they have the money to build one.

2. *The status of clergy is important.*
    Leaders of sects get little public esteem compared with clergy of mainline churches; they do not figure on the mayor's invitation list. Further, because they will probably be dependent upon the giving of the congregation, they are not well paid and have less freedom of action. Life is harder for them and their families, particularly because they are expected to be examples to the flock and live by the rigorous lifestyle and rules which the sect demands.

3. *The educational level of the congregation rises.*
    The founders of the sect may be content with the preaching that first touched them, but their children want ministers to be at least as well educated as themselves.[30] Further, the lowering of boundaries brings their ministers into contact

with other clergy and they feel ill-educated in the presence of the latter. Many embark on further academic study and proudly display their degrees and diplomas.

4. *A sense of history begins to intervene.*

In the early days the appeal of the new and experimental and untried was a powerful motive. But now members want to see themselves as an offshoot of something deeper and wider. They begin to define themselves as a part of the historical tradition of the Church, often seeing their role as restoring something which has been lost. They trawl through the historical records to see earlier examples of their insight. Thus the writings of St Augustine were frequently cited by the leaders of the Reformation. In England, Protestants looked back to a mythical visit by Joseph of Arimathea[31] and the Catholics cited the Venerable Bede. The charismatic movement trawled early Church history to find examples of speaking in tongues.

5. *Apologetics makes an entrance.*

Members of the sect begin to want a clarification of the boundary. What is it that makes them special? How can they explain themselves to their neighbours? Sect leaders need to present the reason for their distinctiveness to others. They need to set out what Berger and Luckmann describe as the 'symbolic universe' which helps their members to 'conceive of their life enfolding in a universe whose ultimate coordinates are known'.[32] The boundary has to be more closely defined and what makes them different from others has to be clarified. Testimony is no longer sufficient.

6. *The cost becomes too high.*

To belong to a sect means a great deal in terms of time and energy as well as money. Initially this was a cost members were happy to pay, but it becomes excessive in the long run. Some, especially among the leaders, suffer from 'burn-out' a state of long-term depression and disenchantment.

However, far more try to restore a balance to their life. Outside interests once again become important: they become less committed to the sect. Initially the 'fellowship of believers' was their 'primary' group and their new symbolic universe enabled them to see life in a new perspective and it was for a time the centre of their existence. But the passage of years makes them realise that there is a world of possibilities outside the church which cannot be ignored.[33] Indeed for some it becomes merely one organisation they belong to, along with several others. Some even drop away altogether. If a movement can sustain a sense of drive and freshness then members are caught into its life, particularly if it is seen to be careful of their personal lives and does not demand more than is reasonable. When groups 'forget why they are doing anything and lose their vision of Jesus Christ of the whole world'[34] they drift into irrelevance in the minds of their members and eventually are discarded. The old rocket which gave glory to the whole of their lives has burnt itself out and is now just a cold, rain-soaked stick with no more power.

What is true of religious organisations is true of other bodies which seek to capture people's enthusiasm. Political parties can offer a vision of a bright new future, which the reality of power soon dissipates. Ecological protests try to change the world but can end in a sense of futility. Entrepreneurs can work round the clock to initiate a business but find that the routine of running it ten years later is less stimulating.

7. *Growth in numbers brings inevitable change.*
The early close fellowship is diluted by the newcomers. A person can feel close to twenty or thirty gathered in a small room: it is less easy to feel as intimate with hundreds of others in an auditorium. The organisation has to grow in order to avoid chaos. There is a need for records and budgets and subscription lists (especially when it becomes necessary to employ people). Its original meeting place is

too small and it starts thinking of new premises. Bureaucracy has begun. This is not necessarily bad – just inevitable.

The search for authority

Part of the process of routinisation is the desire to be accepted by society as the boundary becomes lower. The inevitable question from outsiders is the one posed to Christ: 'By what authority are you doing these things?'[35] Most religions have replied to the question by investing certain writings, rituals or symbols with particular significance. This process is often hastened by internal or external pressures. The need for a Christian canon was made more urgent after Marcion produced his 'truncated canon' in c.150. The Jewish faith had virtually closed the canon by the end of the first century AD in reponse to the destruction of Jerusalem and the scattering of the Jews in 70 AD.[36] The Qur'an, the Vedas, the Buddhist Pali canon, the Book of Mormon and the writings of Ellen White all bear witness to this desire to have an authoritative text.

But it is not only written words that carry authority. Consider the potency of *symbolism*, which is conjured up by the gravity carried by such words as 'crown', 'altar', 'the Speaker's Chair', 'national anthem'. Clifford Geertz says that symbols are 'concrete embodiments of ideas, attitudes, judgements, longings or beliefs . . . they synthesise a people's ethos – the tone, character, and quality of their life, its moral and aesthetic style and mood – and their world view'.[37] An attack on a symbol is seen as an assault on what it represents – whether it is the burning of a country's flag or sacrilege within a church.

The same is true of *ritual*, which Geertz describes as 'consecrated behaviour'. A sacrament is fundamentally an action, sometimes accompanied by words. Religious sacraments are actions performed in concert with others: they define boundaries, produce a common behaviour pattern when believers are in contact with the holy, and remind those present of a wider fellowship. Even the most spontaneous action becomes ritualised. The Eucharist enables the participant to become identified with the death and resurrection of Jesus through a meal whose symbolism both recalls the past and gives strength for the present. Its power comes as much from familiarity as novelty. Symbolism can be more powerful than words. Paul found the struggle over the issue of circumcision to be more violent than debate about points of doctrine.

Social issues

Sociologists insist that religious renewals are always the result of the work of the lower ranks of society. Thus Troeltsch states:

> The really creative, church forming, religious movements are the work of the lower strata. Here only can one find that union of unimpaired imagination, simplicity in emotional life, unreflective character of thought, sponta-neity of energy and vehement force of need, out of which an unconditional faith in a divine revelation, the naiveté of complete surrender and the intransigence of certitude can rise.

Whether the 'lower strata' would recognise themselves in that eulogy is doubtful, but the point is made. A sect by its nature is radical and hence can be linked with those forces in a society which are opposed to authority. As a sect matures into a church it becomes dependent upon affirmation from those in authority and hence less radical in outlook.

It is not difficult to think of examples of such a process. Paul himself glories in the Corinthian church, 'not many of you were wise by human standards, not many were powerful, not many were of noble birth'.[38] The early Methodists were known for their ill-education and their roughness of manner. Further, the history of Methodism, at least in the UK and the US, suggests that many Methodists became 'upwardly mobile'.

Does this apply to all renewals at all times? Does it apply to the monastic renewals or such current renewals as Cursillo, or some streams of the charismatic movement which have begun in universities and well-to-do churches around the world? As a generalisation it may well have exceptions. However, it does point to the fact that renewals often have a radical edge and usually pose problems for those in authority.

Leadership

Weber thought that founders of sects had an affinity with religion which had a 'heroic' quality. In a world which was largely tone-deaf they had an ear for the music of the spirit. They were 'virtuosos' whose 'virtuoso charisma' was recognised by others. He instances shamans and prophets, ascetics and visionaries, the Indian Sramana and the Dervishes. They are regarded as being particularly in touch with the divine and are seen as examples and as leaders. It is their personality and teaching that gives unity and motivation to the movement which collects around them. Modern instances abound, from Charles Taze Russell of the Jehovah's Witnesses to Ron Hubbard of the Church of Scientology.

Any sect faces dislocation when the revered leader passes from the scene. Weber suggested that the virtuoso charisma was either transferred to a successor (or a group) through some such rite as ordination or it would die.[39] This means that a new 'office charisma' is formed, where those who have inherited the leadership are dependent not upon their personality but upon the tradition which has been handed to them. There are obvious examples in the history of the papacy and of Russian communism after the death of Lenin. Weber traces many disputes as being clashes between 'office charisma' and 'virtuoso charisma': the former hardens into a tradition and in its turn becomes resistant to the virtuosos. The sect has become a church.

Dissonance theory

In 1956 Leon Festinger[40] sought to understand the psychological reactions when a prophecy was not fulfilled. In particular he studied a group called the Seekers. Their leader claimed to have received messages from flying saucers saying that there was to be a great flood on December 21st next in Lake City. The group tried to tell others to beware. The date came and went and the Seekers, instead of retiring to lick their wounded pride, were invigorated and became even more evangelistic.

Festinger saw this reaction as arising from a clash between their behaviour and their belief. A person may well know that smoking does them harm and at heart wish to give it up. However, they fail because their addiction is stronger than their will-power. It is often found in such cases that the greater the wish to renounce smoking the greater will be the person's public defence of their right to smoke. In the same way an unfulfilled prophecy will obviously be a crisis point for the sect which prophesied that it would happen. If the commitment of the group to each other and to the belief in fulfilment of the prophecy is deep they may be driven to even greater efforts in an attempt to deny the significance of what had happened (or, usually, what had failed to happen). This does not mean that such people are denying that the prophecy was not fulfilled, but rather that, while accepting that fact, they are denying that it is a challenge to their belief system.

The Millerites after 'The Great Disappointment' of 1843–44, and numerous Jewish messianic groups like the Sabbati Zevi, expanded their work afterwards despite the apparent failure. The Jehovah's Witnesses have given a multiplicity of possible dates for the return of Christ or the beginning of the new millennium, among them 1874, 1914 ('the establishment of God's Kingdom'), 1918 ('God destroys the churches wholesale'), 1925 ('the completion of all things'), and 1975. The last is of particular interest. It was decided in 1966 that the second coming was going to happen in 1975. *Kingdom Ministry* stated in 1968: 'Just think, brothers, there are only about ninety months before 6000 years of man's existence on earth is completed'. Later issues spoke of 'brothers selling their homes and property' and of Witnesses giving their canned goods to neighbours since they would not be needing them. After 1975 had passed uneventfully there were many mutterings and it was announced that '29,893 were disfellowshipped last year'.[41] The sect had become a church as far as some of the supporters were concerned and they were not prepared to accept all that they were told from their Brooklyn headquarters. However, the bulk of Witnesses still saw it as a sect, and, as dissonance theory predicted, their evangelistic zeal increased. As Barbara Harrison says of them:

> The Witnesses had nowhere else to go. Their investment in their religion was total; to leave it would have meant emotional and spiritual bankruptcy. They were not equipped to function in a world without certainty. It was their life. To leave it would be a death.[42]

The effect of growth

When an organisation grows to the size where responsibility has to be delegated then the growth of bureaucracy is inevitable. The movement then changes its direction. It begins to have employees who may well lose the original radical thrust and become more absorbed in maintaining their organisation.

Moreover, as the original fire dies down, many in a movement settle down to 'just being a member'. They find it increasingly difficult to make their voice heard because there are so many fellow-members. Large churches find it difficult to energise their members, who are happy to come regularly and enjoy the fellowship and the worship but feel less incentive to give sacrificially of time or money. As Archbishop Runcie said, they become a church where 'there are too many passengers who should be pilgrims'.

Growth also tends to lower the boundary between the movement and the society it is in: radicalism changes into respectability. Robert Michel's study of this process in the trade unions shows how the movement changed from a time when trade union membership was ridiculed and costly in terms of jobs and acceptance in society, to the leaders partaking of 'beer and sandwiches at Number 10' because the movement had grown to such an extent that it was a force to be reckoned with.

It is noticeable how the recent decline in membership has been accompanied by both a distancing from centres of power and also a raising of the boundary between movement and society: it is no longer quite so respectable to be a trade union member and it can lead to suspicion in the workplace and even dismissal.

Differentiation

A central feature of the development of modern societies is 'differentiation'. Increasing complexity means that societies fragment. A medieval village would have had maybe five or six sorts of job: blacksmith, miller and so on. A modern city has tens of thousands, each with its own pattern of working. Different groupings have their own culture – and sometimes their own religion. Social differentiation thus produces pluralism and this in turn leads to many kinds of beliefs.

The ordinary person in an urban society is confronted by 'a wide variety of religions and other reality-defining agencies that compete for his allegiance or at least attention, and none of which is in a position to coerce him into allegiance'.[43]

NEW RELIGIOUS MOVEMENTS

Emotion swirls around the subject of New Religious Movements (NRMs). Are they a danger to the world? Are they satanic? Are they simply the harmless working out of fantasy? Are they a major threat to the Church – or do they demonstrate the shortcomings of the Church?

A very small number are undoubtedly a threat. Martin Hubback says:

> Only a small minority of unorthodox religious groups represent any danger to society, but those that do are capable of wreaking havoc out of all proportion to their size or importance ... It is the combination of individuals belonging to a group without rational ends, who are not

in a bargaining relationship with the authorities, who are
reckless as to their own survival and who possess the
ability and inclination to use hitherto taboo methods of
destruction, which make cults such a serious threat to
society.[44]

Sometimes they are a danger only to themselves. The Jonestown
mass suicide involved only sect members. The Order of the
Solar Temple grouping killed one another in 1994. The Califor-
nian group thought that by massacring each other they could
be transported to the comet Hale-Bopp to meet King Arthur.

Other NRMs pose a danger to others. The attack using nerve
gas by the Aum Shinrikyo sect on the Japanese underground
in 1995 killed twelve and injured 5,500.[45] Various other NRMs
have ideas about provoking violence in order to accelerate the
coming of some apocalyptic vision.

These groups have different pedigrees. Some come from Sikh,
Hindu or Islamic contexts. Many have Christian backgrounds.
Some arise in fundamentalist settings, like David Koresh of
the Branch Davidians who was a member of the Seventh Day
Adventists, though another, James Jones, was a liberal Christian
who had been previously much involved in social action. The
Falun Gong movement emerged from Buddhism and has grown
fast enough to be perceived as a challenge to the government
of China.[46]

But these are only the few NRMs which attract understandably lurid headlines. There are many, many thousands in the
world. However, the numbers of their members are often exaggerated. For example, it was claimed in the press that there
were 10,000 Hare Krishna members in Toronto – the actual
figure was 80. Some groups vastly exaggerate their membership: the Church of Scientology once claimed half a million,
when the reality was 45,000.

Although many NRMs die out, usually through the death or
failure of their founders, the numbers of such groups are almost
certainly growing. They are no new phenomenon, however:
indeed the term 'New Religious Movement' can be seriously

misleading, since many have been around for decades if not centuries. The term 'New Age' was used by the Theosophical Society in Victorian times, and spiritualists spoke of 'channelling' at least as early as 1881. The pseudo-scientific sects had been around long enough for Jung to say in 1933, 'the passionate interest in these movements arises undoubtedly from psychic energy which can be no longer invested in obsolete forms of religion . . . they have a truly religious character, even if they pretend to be scientific'.

There are various reasons for this recent increase. Some are obvious. The greater ability to communicate through print and television, and now through the Internet, means that potential NRM members can be more easily reached and recruited. Some movements are experts in modern advertising techniques and the manipulation of the media,[47] and the very oddness of some of the NRMs feeds a media constantly looking for quirkiness rather than the ordinary.

More significant may be the changes in outlook which are current in many societies across the globe. Secularisation has led, not so much to atheism, but to the readiness of people, in Chesterton's phrase, 'to believe in anything'. What has been described as the 'smorgasbord of ideas' has led to the growth of the good and the bad and the indifferent. It seems that in Western society it is particularly the intellectually unanchored who are most likely to become NRM members: Eileen Barker, who has made a particular study of such people says that they have a 'disproportionate number of materially advantaged middle-class followers'. The weakness of the mainstream religions has meant that new ideas have no check. Philip Hammond points out that when traditional religions are strong, new ideas are expressed in terms of schism within that religion, but when they are weak new religions form.[48]

In the thought patterns of the Western World there has been a flight from rationality and logic is distrusted. The scientist is suspect. Post-modernism in its many fuzzy guises has allowed people to think beyond the boundaries. In so far as it has created space for humanity, laughter and emotion it has much to commend it, but its scepticism about reason has opened the door to a flood of the weird and the incoherent. Nowhere is this more evident than when we look at what some people believe.

The subject of NRMs is vast and important. For the purposes of this book it is useful to see what categorisations can be discovered. Many renewal movements contain elements of these features – some of them legitimate by Christian standards, others not. Among the many thousands of NRMs there are many exceptions to these categories but the following emphases have emerged:

1. *Some NRMs concentrate on an interior journey.*
    Groups which claim to realise human potential are multi-tudinous, particularly those begun in North America. The heart of much New Age thinking is that there is a spiritual reality within the individual and only in the reintegration of the spiritual and the material can there be an end to personal disharmony. Often this is tied in with some form of attachment to a guru or counsellor who becomes the guide and upon whom the NRM member can become all too dependent. These movements have rightly been called 'self-religions'.

    > The highly privatised culture and the proliferation of choice inspire many people to make their spiritual jour-neys through a pick 'n mix approach ... In a stressful world, self-esteem and self-worth may be the driving factors in developing spirituality, and these may be allied to a need to feel good about one's bodily health, appearance and sexuality.[49]

    There is some evidence that these NRMs are attractive to those who find the adult world frightening and wish to retreat from reality into the only reality they are sure of – themselves.[50]
    The Christian faith, and many other faiths as well, deplores the sort of self-absorption and self-centredness

which this approach leads to. The words of Christ about the need 'to lose life and not to save it' is an immediate rebuke. The Bible asks us to look outwards to God and to the world, not into the mirror. The 'cure of souls' has a long and honourable history and professional counsellors and Christian spiritual directors well know the dangers of over-indulgent introspection and of excessive dependency upon a spiritual guide. Nevertheless it is likely that some forms of Christian renewal can fall into the dangers of encouraging what used to be called 'pride' and this produces an unhealthy relationship between the counsellor and the one receiving help.

2. *Some NRMs are devoted to physical healing.*
   This is a sub-set of (1) since it is centred upon the self, but involves fascination with physical wholeness. This may have a psychological element but is often almost entirely physical. Some forms of alternative medicine or even systems of dieting have a religious character, not only making claims for healing the body but having a philosophy behind them which is part of the package. In Phillip Hammond's words, they provide 'cosmologies, rituals, a language for the interpretation of believer's worlds, a social context for belief and practice, and a group of fellow-believers'.

3. *Some NRMs are pseudo-scientific.*
   Such groups as the Church of Scientology claim that they are based on scientific fact rather than the usual transcendental appeal of a religion. Alongside that are the many NRMs which claim to provide some form of therapeutic community and through which it is argued that members benefit through some pattern of healing based on psychological insights.

4. *Some NRMs seek to copy past religions.*
   Whether it involves followers of Wicca pretending to recreate some pre-Christian nature religion, adherents of

Odinism worshipping the old Norse gods, or those who look to shamans and others who try to continue the religions of previous peoples, the appeal of the past is considerable. Many people yearn for a golden age when human beings and nature lived in harmony and there were no wars or hatred. This view is often foisted on the supposedly peace-loving Celts, though it is doubtful if the Celts themselves would have recognised this image – they themselves conquered many peoples in the centuries before Christ. There is inevitably a sense either of pretence or of antiquarianism in such NRMs.

The Christian Church is not devoid of this longing for the past. Many local churches look back to a time when things were better than the present, and many Christians hanker after some period in the past when all was supposedly good. Whether the New Testament Church can bear the weight which is often put upon it is dubious, and different ages have looked back to the Early Fathers, the medieval Church and the Church of the Reformation as the time when all was well.

5. *Some NRMs major on the bizarre.*
Astrology, crystals, feather divination, UFOs – groups devoted to these and a host of other phenomena exist on the edges of the New Religious Movements. Their appeal is considerable and their potential dangers substantial. Too many people allow their horoscope to dictate their lives and too many are drawn by the lure of the fantastic into dangerous waters. Often they are in fashion for a time only to lose their status to another, even more offbeat, belief system. At the time of writing, the followers of Ellen Greve (who calls herself Jasmuheen) claim that it is possible to live without food or drink, but no doubt many others will have passed through the media spotlight by the time you read these words.

It is on the fringe of this fringe that there exist those who exchange evil for good, who seek to worship Satan or indulge in acts of ritual violence. This may be allied to political ends, as in the American far-right groups who indulge in violent racism under the pretence of maintaining a Christian civilisation (represented in the Ku Klux Klan by the burning cross). Often these groups are led by people with a charismatic but warped personality or by those with mental disorders.

CONCLUSION

The insights of the sociologists are certainly of value as we look at some of the ways in which renewal has been handled within the Church. In addition, the NRMs provide us with a kaleido-scopic view of the sane and the insane, the dotty and the deadly dangerous: they can provide us with examples of how people act when they are part of a sect.

3 Renewal in the Temple

We have now set out the hypothesis and some insights from sociology which can help us to explore renewals more clearly. In the next four chapters we shall look at four periods of church history and then at the contemporary scene which is in the process of becoming history. In each chapter we shall see what we can learn – not to burrow like antiquarians into bygone years but to see what we can deduce for the present.

The New Testament is socketed in the Old. To contemporaries the early Christian Church seemed to be a renewal movement within Judaism.[1] Only later was it clear that it was good news for the whole world, Jew and Gentile alike. The formation of the Church and its development in the New Testament period and beyond is the story of a renewal and we shall have to see if it fits into the hypothesis that has been suggested. In particular we shall look at two groups within the Church which do not feature in the New Testament – the Ebionites and the followers of Montanus – whose history will be especially helpful for us.

We shall look at two elements of the New Testament in particular. The first is the way in which the Church worked – or did not work, for all was by no means perfect in the first-century Church and we can learn as much from its malfunctioning as from what went well. The second is the sociological background which lies behind the New Testament. Gerd Theissen suggests there are three methods of doing this:[2]

(a) *constructive* – direct inferences which can be drawn from the text, e.g. the social stratification in the Corinthian church which can be deduced from 1 Corinthians 11:17ff.

(b)   *analytic* – trying to draw out the implications behind the text. The sociologist 'seeks to identify and investigate conflicts, draws information about operative norms for ethical exhortations . . . and connections between symbolism and experienced reality'.

(c)   *comparative* – comparing New Testament passages with other material. This could come from contemporary history or later, so it might emanate from Qumran or from a sixteenth-century sect.

THE HYPOTHESIS

Stage 1: Renewal

Judaea had once been part of the divided carcass of the empire of Alexander the Great, but Rome had grown in influence until it conquered the area in 63 BC. In 47 BC Julius Caesar had appointed Herod as procurator. By skilful political manoeuvring and by murdering his rivals he established himself as 'King of the Jews' and he, his two sons, his grandson and his great-grandson ruled until about AD 100. Roman officials were appointed as procurators, as was normal with small third-class provinces. Judaea was occupied territory. As so often in such situations, the people's faith became the centre of national resistance, and was intensified by the procurators' ignorance towards the sensibilities of that faith. Pilate antagonised the nation by doing what his predecessors had been too prudent to do, when he put the Roman standards, with images of the Emperor, in the Temple. His weak climb-down after six days indicated to the religious leaders that here they had a man who was vulnerable to pressure. The drama of Good Friday had been foreshadowed.

Into this fiercely nationalistic people, who were resentful yet powerless, Jesus was born. Luke describes his baptism by John briefly but climactically for it was there that 'the Holy Spirit descended upon him in bodily form like a dove'. Then, 'full of the Holy Spirit', he is 'led by the Spirit' into the wilderness. After the temptation, 'filled with the Holy Spirit', he begins to teach in the synagogues – and the first episode is in his own home town.[3] This emphasis on the Spirit is continued in his reading of 'the Nazareth manifesto'[4] which was initially well received. What happened next was not. Jesus went on to quote two Old Testament passages which showed that God cared as much for non-Jews and for non-believers in Yahweh as for Jews. The stories of the widow of Zarephath and of Naaman, if spoken in this way in an orthodox synagogue in Israel today would probably arouse the same hostility. Jesus was driven out and nearly stoned for challenging their racism.[5] The Spirit-filled Jesus taught and worked wonders and spoke of a community of love entered through repentance but also of a world transformed:

> Jesus' Kingdom ministry launches an all out attack on evil in all its manifestations. God's reign arrives when Jesus overcomes the power of evil . . . which takes many forms: pain, sickness, death, demon-possession, personal sin and immorality, the loveless self-righteousness of those who claim to know God, the maintaining of special class privileges, the brokenness of human relationships.[6]

His appeal was to the mass of people and to the religious leaders themselves. But, as had been proclaimed at Nazareth, his ministry was universal. It touched those who were the excluded – the poor and the prostitutes and also those, like the tax-collectors, who had done well out of the Roman occupation. He even leapt over the Jewish/Gentile boundary and helped the Samaritan and the Syro-Phoenician: he even warmly accepted the hated Romans. The crucifixion and the resurrection were the effective signs of this two-pronged ministry which had been heralded in the synagogue at Nazareth – renewal speaks both of suffering and of glory.

Miracles were Jesus' calling-card. The reality of his possession of the Spirit was shown by what he did. 'It is beyond question

that Jesus had powers beyond that of a normal man. Further-
more, he had the gift of arousing these capabilities in others.
His followers had performed miracles themselves. All these
miracles were perceived as signs of the great eschatalogical
revolution.'[7] These were the Johannine 'signs' which pointed
both to the nature of the Kingdom – that it had no boundaries
and that its purpose was restoration – and also to the nature of
Jesus as God's chosen one.

The events of Pentecost showed that the charisma of the
leader (in both the theological and the sociological sense) was
passed to the followers: 'the charismatic community of disciples
is Spirit-empowered and Spirit-directed for its missionary
task'.[8] 'Day by day, they spent much time together in the
Temple . . .' (Acts 2:46). The renewal was still contained within
Judaism, but the nature of the message meant that it was bound,
sooner or later, to break through that boundary.

Stage 2: Conflict

Renewals are born in conflict. Jesus said his Kingdom 'was not
of this world' but it inevitably clashed with the kingdoms of
this world. In Judaea it encountered two areas of power – the
religious authorities and the Romans. Later it collided with
the philosophies and world-views of the Graeco-Roman world.

The religious authorities were well used to dealing with this
sort of difficulty. Swift political action soon led to the crucifixion
of the leader. The High Priests probably prided themselves on
their decisiveness in dealing with the matter within a week of
its escalation to danger level. It was clear that there were still
some of the man's followers around and there was the question
as to how they should be dealt with. When the authorities took
council together, Gamaliel was able to cite the case of Theudas
'claiming to be somebody' who led a rising, and also Judas the
Galilean who 'got people to follow him' (Acts 5:33–42). But
neither event had come to anything and, Gamaliel suggested,
precipitate action would not be sensible now. Like any committee, the Council relished the idea of doing nothing: besides,

now that the leader had been accounted for it was probable that the movement would disintegrate like so many before it.

At first there was considerable tolerance of the growing infant Church. Its followers were not thrown out of the Temple and Luke records that 'a great many of the priests became obedient to the faith' (Acts 6:7). It was only when 'the synagogue of the Freedmen'[9] clashed with Stephen some years after Jesus' crucifixion and instigated his trial before the Council that positions hardened. However, even after Stephen's martyrdom it is clear that persecution was limited to Jerusalem, for the Christians 'except the apostles' were scattered only as far as Judaea and Samaria (Acts 8:1), i.e. into the countryside around the capital. When Paul and his companions travelled out into the Gentile world it was to the synagogues that they went first, and they seem to have been welcomed and given freedom to speak.

Gradually positions hardened. The renewal began to be seen by Jews as something which was not just a renewal within Judaism but a cuckoo in their nest. The divisions inevitably intensified when the Jews were fighting for their lives as the Roman armies sought to crush the whole nation in AD 66–70. That Christians were excluded from the synagogues in AD 85 is not surprising. What may be unexpected is the tolerance shown by the Jewish authorities for so long.

Relations with the Roman authorities were initially good. Pilate's dithering and his eventual agreement to the crucifixion of Jesus was probably seen by his superiors as typical of a procurator with poor political judgement – assuming that such a minor event had come to their ears at all. In Acts the Romans are shown as competent, fair-minded and generally acting to protect Christians from mob violence.[10] In the Epistles they are to be prayed for and their God-given role in keeping order in society is underlined. Yet the Book of Revelation portrays Rome as Babylon, a representation of all human society organised in opposition to God, for which a terrible fate is reserved.[11] In part this may have been because Nero for political reasons wanted a scapegoat after the fire of Rome.[12] In part, too, it was because any society seems to need a despised group to abominate or mock and the Christians were available to fill this role. It may also have been that they were still linked with the Jews in the minds of the Roman authorities, and as these were in revolt against the emperor Christians were therefore both to be feared as possible subversives and also to be ostracised. Another factor was the increasing cult of the emperor: Domitian (81–96) called himself 'Master and God' and demanded allegiance. Neither Jews nor Christians would acknowledge this and there was widespread and direct persecution of those who would not burn a pinch of incense on the altar of the emperor.

Certainly from the 60s and 70s AD there was a marked hardening of official attitudes and by 112 Pliny was writing to the Emperor asking for advice on how to deal with the Christians, who by this time were regarded as enemies of the state. Were they to be executed just for being Christians, he asked; and should he execute the old and the young along with the rest. He had examined two of their women under torture and found nothing very terrible, only 'squalid superstitions'.

The benign Roman rule of Acts had become the whore of Babylon, 'drunk with the blood of the saints and the blood of the witnesses to Jesus'.[13]

Stage 3: Networking

Despite the practical difficulties of travel the first-century Roman Empire was crisscrossed by Christians meeting each other. They visit each other, they write letters, they know about and pray for each other.[14] The letters of the New Testament give us a vivid picture of this: they give greetings and instruction, but also speak of individuals on the move – 'Tychicus will tell you everything', 'I will come to you shortly'. The Synod at Jerusalem must have needed a considerable logistical exercise to gather everyone together.

The early Christians met in order to receive support from each other, to be reassured that they were not alone and that there were more and more 'colonies of heaven' being planted, and that the Christian faith was going forward. The whole story of Acts is of the success of the faith spiralling in towards the greatest city in the world.

As Christians met they began, like any group of people, to acquire a language peculiar to themselves. New words were created, old words were given new meanings. The New Testament is full of examples of this. *Kopos* normally meant hard menial and physical work; Paul invests it with a much more distinguished significance – his *kopos* was to 'present everyone mature in Christ'.[15] *Didache* normally just meant 'instruction', but all strands in the New Testament give it the deeper sense of 'the whole body of teaching'.[16] *Splanchnizomai* meant either eating the offal of a sacrifice or using it in divination; in the New Testament it becomes 'having a deep compassion' for someone.[17] New ideas struggled to be expressed and pushed out the boundaries of the dictionary. These words became the common currency of the infant Church, so that Paul could use them in writing to the different churches knowing that he would be understood.

Inevitably networking means that certain people become recognised as leaders. We know of Peter, Paul, Barnabas and the others named in the New Testament, but there must have been many others who were leaders of local churches and some who were known more widely. They did not always agree. Paul had public disagreements with Peter and with Barnabas. The 'super-apostles' tried to usurp Paul's position. Renewals always throw up leaders, and the sheer excitement and the intoxicating flow of new ideas mean that they look at things differently. Authority begins to become an issue. By now it is a couple of decades or more after Pentecost: the Christian renewal has begun to enter the second generation – one of the most dangerous phases for any movement. It is the time when, in a local church, the original leader goes, or in a sect the guru leaves the scene, or the leaders with charisma grow old and retire.

Authority

It happened in New Testament times; it happens still. Questions
about authority are the most difficult that any renewal has to
face, and unless they are resolved the renewal will either fragment endlessly, or peter out into nothingness. The Didache is
a sort of handbook on church order. Like most handbooks it
was added to and amended down the years, but probably
it stems from the later years of the first century. When discussing the wandering people who came to the churches
claiming to be prophets or apostles, the question is posed: 'Are
these people true or fake?' The Church needs to be protected
from the 'false prophets and corrupters'. The Didache gives a
list of tests: e.g. 'Do they ask for money?', 'Do they stay too
long?', 'Is their behaviour according to their teaching?' Clearly
it was a major problem and one text suggests that Christians
would be sensible to 'appoint for yourselves bishops and
deacons worthy of the Lord . . . for unto you they also perform
the service of the prophets and teachers'. In other words, it is
better to have people you know than some of these wanderers
whose credentials you are unsure about.[18]

The same process can be seen in the Pastoral Epistles. There,
a growing sense of order can be perceived: there are now
deacons and bishops and they need to have certain qualifi-
cations. One requirement is a good name outside the Church
(1 Tim. 3:7) – an indication of the more settled status of the
Church within society. In sociological terms, the boundary is
being lowered and the world outside the Church is not being
seen as totally evil. Further, all leaders are not equal – some
are paid at least an honorarium, and the important ones get a
double 'honour' (1 Tim. 5:17).[19] Earlier, as Margaret MacDonald
stresses, 'the Pauline church is composed of nothing except
laymen, who nevertheless are all, within their possibilities, at
the same time priests and office-holders . . . instruments of the
Spirit for the enactment of the Gospel in the everyday world'.[20]
Paul had boasted to both the Ephesian and the Corinthian
churches that he had received nothing from them (Acts 20:34;

1 Cor. 4:12). By the time of the Pastorals some of the ministers
were stipendary.

Inevitably, the regular pastoral and teaching ministry, which
is envisaged for people like Timothy, plays down the occasional,
potentially disruptive ministry of the prophet. 'The seeds of
church order already sown, grow into a pattern of ministry
which . . . inevitably did quench the prophetic spirit at work
within the whole body of Christ.'[21] As we shall see, the Montanist movement was an attempt to restore the prophetic
ministry to its former status.

It has been argued that in the days immediately after Pentecost there were no authority structures in the Spirit-filled
community, but this is too simplistic a view.[22] There were
structures which were sometimes based on a close family
relationship with Jesus, like that of James the Just, or close
personal relationships like those of the Apostles. Others, like
Barnabas, through their personality, energy and wisdom were
perceived to have the gift of leadership. In the early stage where
churches were being planted the person who came with the
gospel was inevitably regarded as having a unique position as
trail blazer.[23] However, with the passage of time local churches
wanted more say in who should lead them and they were
becoming more critical. Paul's absences were resented and this
made the likelihood of the development of a parallel leadership
almost inevitable. Timothy faced questions because of his youth.
The wandering ministry seen in the Didache came to be
regarded as too uncertain for regular worship and teaching.
The stage was set for the establishing of bishops, elders and
deacons.

Boundaries had to be protected. The need for discipline inevitably led to the need for responsible people to exercise it.
Whether it was the charismatic leadership of Peter in relation
to Ananias and Sapphira in Acts 5 or the formal excommunication of the impenitent commanded by Paul in 1 Corinthians
5:3–5, some came to be regarded as having authority to set the
boundary – in relation both to sinful behaviour and to doctrinal
standards. The leader had become judge.

An interesting change of nomenclature takes place. *Episcopos* (bishop) and *presbuteros* (elder) are at first used interchangeably to refer to the same people. However *presbuteros*, the term normally used in the Early Church for a leader, has its roots in the Jewish faith and has a primarily religious connotation: the Sanhedrin was composed of the 'elders of Israel' and synagogues came to be governed by elders. However, increasingly Church leaders came to be referred to as *episkopoi* rather than *presbuteroi* and this word has a primarily secular significance. It was used for Greek officials, especially if they had responsibility for public funds. It was even used for secret policemen![24] The structure of the Church had begun to ape secular society rather than its Jewish fountainhead – an accommodation which was to be copied many times in the future. This showed a Church more at ease in its surroundings.

But approved leaders by themselves could not answer all questions. There had to be an authoritative source which would act as a yardstick. The bishops, now leaders of local churches or groups of churches, began to defer to those who were more experienced or perceived to have greater wisdom. Thus Dionysus of Corinth (c. AD 170) was asked for advice by several churches in the area of the Aegean. Churches in some major cities were seen as more prestigious than others. With the destruction of Jerusalem and the apparent weakness of the church in Athens, the torch inevitably passed to the Bishop in Rome. But who was the Bishop of Rome? Irenaeus (c. AD 180) supplies lists of the Bishops of Rome back to the Apostles so that churches elsewhere could be assured of the authority of the person they were seeking help from.[25]

But a human authority was not enough. There had to be a written one as well. The Greek word *kanon* means 'measuring rod' or 'list'. The canon of Scripture took many years to evolve in its entirety,[26] but authoritative writings were accepted at a very early date. The epistles of Paul seem to have almost immediately achieved a status far beyond the church they had been addressed to, and the four gospels were widely accepted by the beginning of the second century.

The Church now had an authoritative book and the arguments about the ideas we now call heresies were conducted before a court of final appeal. The exact exegesis of the Bible, of course, remained a matter for conjecture. It was through these debates that the Church came to define its belief.

Stage 4: Definition

The early Christian renewal movement within Judaism immediately began to show how far its followers were both the same as and yet different from other Jews. Stephen's defence before the Sanhedrin in Acts 7 may represent a common early Christian apologetic: he rehearses the history of the Jewish nation and then moves to the Old Testament passages which seem to deny the need for temple and ritual sacrifice. The common ground which all Jews share is recounted before the controversial issues are raised. In particular the claim to the messiahship of Jesus and God's acceptance of that claim by his resurrection were seen as the divisive issues to be introduced at the end of the discourse.

With the move into the Gentile world the Church had to determine more closely what should be the core of its teaching. How much Jewishness from the Old Testament needed to be retained, how much needed to be modified and how much completely new material should be added? It was here that the genius of Paul guided the Church. He wrestled with the relation of the Church and Judaism, supremely in Romans 9–11, but he went beyond merely showing how the Christian faith was different from Judaism. He built upon the life and teachings of Jesus a great intellectual cathedral which began to define more fully the relation of human beings and God. He further began to spell out who Jesus of Nazareth was and what was the significance of his life. He set out the relationships which should exist within the Church and he began to analyse more closely the boundaries between the Church and the world. It was an awe-inspiring, Spirit-inspired feat which meant that the Church was able to stand confidently before the Gentile world without being dependent upon the Jewish mother who had given birth to the Christian faith.

Paul was not, of course, alone in this, but there is no doubt that his analytical tour de force was foundational in establishing the Church as a body that had credibility in the Graeco-Roman world, showing it to be not just a Jewish sect but a formidable spiritual and intellectual force. His work was carried on by others and it was said of Origen (c.185–c.254) that he was the first systematic theologian. In particular Paul's successors integrated Christianity with Greek philosophy. Initially regarded with some contempt by Greek philosophers, the Christian faith by the sixth century came to dominate the intellectual landscape to such an extent that non-Christians were despised as *barbaroi*, and only Christians were regarded as civilised. How helpful this development was to the reality behind the meticulously defined words is questionable. Van der Aalst sums up the process: 'the message became doctrine, the doctrine dogma, and this dogma was expounded in precepts which were expertly strung together'.[27]

But definition was not required only in relation to the world outside the Church. There were those within who needed further explanation of their faith. Christopher Rowland says that Paul's epistles are 'proof of the need for legitimation and to explain the content of revelation to members of the sect with a view to accounting for their behaviour to the outside world (eg. 1 Cor 7.12–16 concerning marriage partners, and passim in explanation to Jews about the Law).'[28]

Sociologically speaking, there was a need for 'universe maintenance'. With the growth of a new generation and a lessening of the original eschatalogical urgency there were the dangers of deviance. Church members in Colossae were exhorted not to move 'from the hope promised by the gospel you heard' (Col. 1:23), nor to allow those with exotic ascetic ideas to 'disqualify' them and move them from allegiance to 'the head' (2: 16–19). Additionally, they were not to let others take them 'captive through philosophy and empty deceit, according to human tradition . . . and not according to Christ' (2:8). To counter these tendencies Paul wrote his epistles, and it was his longing to care for these new Christians which gives his letters so much of their urgency and emotional power.

Paul did not only use words to get his message across. He showed that he was a Spirit-filled person. As Christopher Rowland says, 'he transmits his gospel not only verbally but through pneumatic acts'. Paul says his message was not 'in words only but with power and the Holy Spirit and with full conviction' (1 Thess. 1:5; cf. Rom. 15:19; 1 Cor. 2:4). He was no stranger to mystical experiences (2 Cor. 12:12; 1 Cor. 2:4) and he possessed the gifts of tongues (1 Cor. 14:18) and prophecy (1 Thess. 3:4). He expected these manifestations to continue in churches even when he was not with them, even in those churches which were wobbling into heresy (Gal. 3:5).

However, more detailed definition was required when other challenges arose. The succession of 'heresies' during the first four centuries meant that the Christian faith had to be more and more exact in its definition. Further, as the gospel entered the Roman world it encountered a cast of mind which demanded verbal precision: the Greeks had been content to outline the mystery with less credal exactitude. The Jewish world of the New Testament had seen 'truth' conveyed by many means:

(a) by emotions leading to *metanoia* – a change of heart as well as a change of mind;

(b) by signs and wonders;

(c) by the nature of the Christian fellowship;

(d) by subliminal osmosis through worship in the Temple, and subsequently in Christian gatherings;

(e) by oral teaching, often in the form of stories and parables.

When Paul and others set out propositional statements to define the faith more closely, this was seen as only one of several means of apprehending truth. It has been of the greatest disservice to the Church that the demand for pinpoint verbal accuracy became paramount above all other methods of defining and conveying the truth about the Father, Son and

Holy Spirit. The loss of the more holistic Hebraic view of truth which fills both Old and New Testaments and its replacement by the Roman demand for exactitude of doctrinal statements was deep and lasts to this day.

Of particular interest in studying this process are the Montanists – the first real renewal movement within Christianity.[29] Here we are more concerned with how the main body of the Church dealt with a threat to its own definition of itself by an enthusiastic sect, than in the details of Montanist beliefs and history.

Montanism

By the middle of the second century the Christian faith had made remarkable inroads into the Gentile world. It was an established part of the social scenery in many parts of the Roman Empire, though stronger in the towns and cities than in the countryside. However the spiritual temperature had dropped: Church order had become more important than the free life of the Spirit, and there was little sense of the immediacy and urgency which had flowed from the eschatology of the Early Church. Moreover, the hard incarnational edge of the Christian faith had tended to become lost in speculative metaphysics and the allegorical interpretation of Scripture. There was little emphasis upon the coming of the Kingdom and more upon individual moralism.

Montanus gave his name to the 'New Prophecy', a movement which began in the rural uplands of Asia Minor and which spread widely. It preached an earthenware gospel in comparison with the carefully crafted bone china of contemporary theology. The Age of the Son had now given way to the Age of the Spirit; the millennial rule of Christ was soon to begin with the descent of the Heavenly Jerusalem near Pepuza in Phrygia; the prophets and prophetesses (there were many women involved) were the messengers of God; tongues and other charismatic gifts were to be exercised. The movement demanded a life lived according to strict rules – purity in sexual relationships, much penitential fasting, steadfastness in times of persecution. They had no doubt about their own superiority to other Christians – they were the *pneumatikos pneumatike* – 'spiritual Christians for other spiritual Christians'. About AD 200 they gained their most prestigious convert, Tertullian,[30] and in 203 their most famous martyrs, Perpetua and Felicity.

Reactions to Montanism have varied. 'Of whatever century, and whether catholic or protestant, writers have tended to treat Montanism with a sideways glance at the Reformation.'[31] This is not surprising since questions about authority, the ministry of women, the validity of charismata and the nature of prophecy are all raised by any study of Montanism.

The contemporary Church dealt with this invasion of enthusiasm by a number of tactics:

1. The Church answered the ultimate question – was Montanism a genuine manifestation of the Holy Spirit? – with a definite 'No'. Some assigned the movement to the work of the devil, while others looked to a more human source: like Edward Gibbon speaking of the whirling dervishes, they in effect claimed that the Montanists 'mistake the giddiness of the head for the illumination of the spirit'.

2. Personal attacks were made upon the leaders, especially Montanus himself. It was claimed that he was a recent convert to Christianity, that he operated in a frenzy akin to that of the followers of heathen gods and that he benefited financially from the movement.

3. The homespun theology which they preached was belittled. Behind some of this is the superiority assumed by the urban over the rural. The Montanists were called by the Latin word *paganus*. It means 'peasant', 'yokel', 'villager' – essentially uneducated and ill-informed compared to the sophisticated way of life and thinking of city dwellers.[32] Montanists came to be regarded as heretics and were denounced at a series of Church Councils. The Council of Iconium in 287 even decreed that they had to be rebaptised if they wished to join a Catholic church.

4. There was a thoroughly misogynistic view of the women

who played a prominent part in the movement. It is possible that they were ordained.[33] Thus Didymus of Alexandria scornfully alluded to the 'disciples of delirious women'.

5. Their practices were mocked by the use of nicknames. They were called *artotyrites* – 'bread and cheesers' – because it was thought they offered bread and cheese to God in their worship. Others called them *tascodrougites* – 'nose-peggers' – (possibly because they passed their hands over their faces as a sign of repentance).

6. The orthodox questioned the source of the charismatic happenings. Some Montanists had claimed that they were not in control when making their prophecies. This led Hippolytus and other critics to assert that prophecies should be under the control of the prophet – they should not be words spoken in a trance like those of the followers of the Greek gods.[34] They criticised the Montanists for their forms of worship which were claimed to be more like the ecstatic worship of pagan gods.

7. While the Montanists paid lip-service to the local bishops, Ignatius complained that in practice their bishops were ignored and the Montanists therefore held 'invalid' meetings. In reality the Montanists saw their own 'Patriarchs of Pepuza' as the ultimate authority.

8. They were condemned as divisive at a time when the unity of Christians was important during a period of persecution. Contemporary disasters within the Empire through plague, earthquakes and barbarian invasion were held to require a more co-operative attitude from the Montanists.

9. It was complained that they did not follow the customs of the wider Church. Thus when the orthodox Christians adjusted the date of Easter in 202 the Montanists did not follow. Inevitably this meant the rift between the two sides widened.

10. Physical violence was used. John of Ephesus went to

Pepuza and burnt the Montanist meeting place and forced open their shrine, despite their tears.

It is difficult to sum up Montanism. Undoubtedly there were elements of fanaticism but it was largely orthodox in belief. For a few centuries it remained on the edge of the Church, repeatedly condemned by Church Councils. Some Montanists joined other groups which also pursued a strict lifestyle and refused readmittance to the church of those who lapsed under persecution. Inevitably what remained of the movement split into smaller and smaller groupings and it is finally heard of late in the fifth century – three hundred years after its birth.

One feature which is illustrated by this review of Montanism is that the methods by which renewals are rubbished by their opponents have been repeated all too many times throughout the history of the Church.

Stage 5: Divergence

Renewals usually have the two components, Strand B and Strand A: there are those people who remain as 'renewalists' within the parent body, and those who leave to form their own organisation. Immediately after Pentecost there was unanimity – Christ's followers were touched by renewal, but they remained practising Jews and they observed the dietary laws,[35] kept the Sabbath and so on. The proclamation of the gospel to the Gentiles and its acceptance by them had been foreshadowed by Christ in his conversation with the centurion in Mark 7: 'I tell you, not even in Israel have I found such faith'. Once the gospel had left the Jewish surroundings of Jerusalem it was bound to be challenged as to its Jewishness. Luke sees Acts 10 as a hinge point in his book, when Peter is given permission by God to break the Jewish rules by eating ritually unclean food. This enables Peter to go to Cornelius and speak to him of Jesus. After that most of Acts takes place outside the Jewish milieu in which it began.

Peter's struggle to overcome his culturally induced emotional reluctance to eat unclean food shows how strong was the hold of the rabbinic law. Immediately he ran into opposition for not all the Jewish Christians had had his experience and while Acts 11 shows that those who heard his testimony were placated, there must have been many who were deeply disturbed as they heard stories of Gentiles being converted and not being instructed to keep the Jewish laws. Not surprisingly circumcision was the key issue. In Acts 11:2 the Jewish critics of the Gentile mission are simply called *'oi ek peritomes'* – 'those of the circumcision': it sounds dangerously like the title of a faction.

Despite Peter's defence the issue remained. News from Cyprus and Asia Minor of the progress of the Gentile mission angered some Jewish Christians to such an extent that they travelled far to meet the Gentile converts and tell them, 'unless you are circumcised according to the custom of Moses, you cannot be saved'.[36] In the end a synod was called in Jerusalem. The result, like many such gatherings in the future of the Church, was an uneasy compromise. A form of words was agreed which was sent to the Gentile Christians; this specified that some of the dietary laws were to be observed and sin was to be avoided. In the nature of such communiqués, what was not said was more important than what was stated. In particular, it did not include any requirement for converts to be circumcised, and so was received with thanksgiving in Gentile Antioch.[37] After that the results of the great synod seem to have been largely forgotten. In his discussion about meat offered to idols Paul makes no reference to it, and the rest of the New Testament is silent.

'Those of the circumcision' were not silenced. They harassed and confused Paul's churches until he was forced to write with his temper barely under control. Finally, in Galatians 5:12 he explodes, 'I wish those who unsettle you would castrate themselves'. It was a classic encounter between Strand A and Strand B. The first felt that those who remained were too subservient to the parent body and were half-hearted, even heretical. Strand B, meanwhile, felt that those who left had strayed much too far away from the tradition and needed to be brought to a more balanced outlook.

The decay of Jewish Christianity

The cradle of the Christian faith was fashioned in Jerusalem. Jesus, the apostles, virtually all the early disciples, were all Jewish. But once the Gentile mission had begun the Jewish Christians became an increasingly smaller proportion of the Church: probably within thirty years of Pentecost, Gentiles out-numbered Jews. What happened all too well illustrates divergence within a renewal.

The Jewish Church had remained, becoming increasingly cut off from the Gentile Church and devastated by the Roman invasion of AD 66. Their temple gone, they seem to have frag-mented into tiny groups and eventually to have disappeared.

In AD 62 the Jewish Church lost its most revered authority, James the Just, the brother of Jesus (Mark 6:3), who was seen by them as the greatest of the early Christian leaders. In AD 70 the soldiers of Vespasian and Titus destroyed the Holy City. The prestige of being the centre of the Christian world passed to Rome. The Christians who survived settled at Pella, on the east bank of the Jordan, and they remained for years largely cut off from the rest of the Church and fragmenting into smaller and smaller sects.

Among these were the Ebionites. The name means, literally, 'the poor ones', probably referring to the first words of the Sermon on the Mount in Aramaic – 'blessed are the poor in spirit'. Hostile Church fathers produced less complimentary derivations, some suggesting that it was because of the poverty of the Jewish law, while Eusebius speculated that it was because they 'held poor and mean opinions of Christ'. Originally the name Ebionite may have referred to all Christians who kept the Jewish law and Justin, in c. 175, describes two outlooks among Jewish Christians – one of which allowed that it was possible to be a Christian without obeying the law, while the other made obedience essential for salvation.

However, as the Jewish Christians fragmented further, the

Ebionite name came to be restricted to certain groups of Jewish Christians. Again, typically in these situations they drifted further and further from mainstream Christian thinking. Living strictly by the Jewish law they deeply regretted the Gentile mission, regarding Paul as 'an apostate from the law' and rejecting all his epistles. The derivation of their name from the Sermon on the Mount in Matthew 5 is significant for they accepted only the gospel of Matthew as authentic.[38] While accepting Jesus as Messiah, they refused to acknowledge his divinity. One Ebionite group accepted the virgin birth and another did not.[39] Curiously, they also taught that both John the Baptist and Jesus were vegetarian – changing John's diet from 'locusts' to 'cake'! Later they seem to have come under gnostic influence and came to believe that salvation was achieved through knowledge (*gnosis*) and baptism, which gave strength to keep the law.

The second century saw the rise of anti-Jewish polemic among Christians, with Origen (c.185–c.254) being particularly hostile. The long history of Christian anti-Semitism had begun and made it emotionally difficult for Gentile Christians to accept as fellow-believers those who were both Christians and Jews.

Epiphanius (c.315–403) mentions that there were still small Ebionite groups in Syria and Judaea, while Jerome (c.345–420) alludes to some reasonably orthodox Jewish Christians he had met during his sojourn as a hermit in the Syrian desert. Afterwards there is nothing but silence as these groups seem to have petered out or been absorbed by other churches. The renewal within Judaism was dead.[40]

Stage 6: Communication

At this stage in the life of a renewal communication between the different elements is essential. In this process it is those in Strand B who are crucial for it is they who understand the thinking of both those in Strand A and also those in the mainstream. They interpret the one to the other.

Sadly, in the life of the Early Church Strand B – the Jewish Christians – had virtually died out as a separate entity. This Strand had become, because of the destruction of Jerusalem, first of all a far-off minority within Christianity and then declined almost to nothing. The few there were spoke a different language and had a very different outlook from the great majority of Christian believers. The Ebionites who were encountered by the majority were regarded as marginally heretical and certainly with nothing to offer the Church.

The result was that Judaism and Christianity lost the possibility of communication, and questions about the relationship of the Old Covenant and the New became marginal. Without Strand B dialogue ceased. About AD 150 Justin Martyr wrote his 'Dialogue with Trypho' which addressed these issues, but this was not what most Christian apologists were writing about: they were encountering the very different and more immediately urgent world of the Greeks and the Romans.[41]

The absence of this dialogue had fateful consequences. The Christian faith lost the respect and understanding it should have had for its Jewish roots and the two faiths settled into a mutual hostility and suspicion.

Stage 7: Consequences

With the split from Judaism complete and with no Strand B, there were two possibilities open to the Early Church. It could fragment or it could form a new faith.

The dangers of fragmentation were very real. Geography made it a distinct possibility – what Christians in the west did was of little significance to those in the east of the Mediterranean. The very enthusiasm of the Christians meant that new ideas were pouring out freely. As different nationalities became Christian, the likelihood increased that they would develop their own form of Christianity, as happened among the Goths. Sporadic persecutions drove Christians underground and made open communication, or even evangelism, difficult.

Paul struggles against these centrifugal forces in his letters

and the Early Church had repeatedly to emphasise its cath-
olicity. Different outlooks and ideas swim across the scene and
have to be met. Histories of the Early Church are full of heresies
which came to the surface and had to be combatted.

It may be regrettable but it is not surprising that the Church
chose to meet this though a growing centralism and authoritarianism. The bishops came to be regarded as the keepers of
the faith and of the unity of the Church, and to bolster their
position extravagant claims were made for their office. But all
bishops were not equal: certain sees became more significant
than others, and as we have seen, Rome became the court of
appeal for many areas.

Church leaders met in order to deal with problems within
the Church and this led to the establishment of Church Councils. They were multitudinous and their deliberations are full
of anathemas against one group or another, condemnation of
non-orthodox opinions and, sometimes, comments of a highly
political nature.

However, while some groups split from the main fellowship
of the faith, the mainstream kept together as one Church.
Without that unity the Church would have found it much
harder to face the break-up of the Roman Empire and the 'Dark
Ages' with the assurance that led it to become the main conduit
of learning and faith. Strand A had become the Church.

CONCLUSIONS

Renewals have to manage cultural transfer successfully[42]

The move from the Jewish matrix to the new Gentile cultural
milieu amply illustrates several points.

1. No renewal is free of cultural accretions and, in the early
    stages at least, the significance of these may not be
    recognised.
2. The culture from which a renewal springs is valuable in
    itself and it is impossible to reject it completely, even if

those involved wish to do so. On the other hand there has to be a sufficient level of tension between the renewal and the mainstream culture if the renewal is to be robust enough to be transferred to another culture.

3. If the transfer is to be completed successfully some of the original cultural accretions have to be dropped. Thus Colossians and Ephesians 'point to a simultaneous appeal to tradition and the transformation of tradition to "fit" a new situation'.[43] Disputes will often spotlight certain issues, such as circumcision, or ritually clean and unclean food.

4. Strand A will tend to be bolder in making these adaptations and this will cause friction with Strand B and even more so with the mainstream. Some in Strand B will feel that the original renewal has been betrayed and try to bring back those in Strand A to the way of the truth as they see it.

5. There may be attempts at a compromise to accommodate both cultures, as at the Jerusalem Synod. However, where there are wide cultural differences, as between the Jewish and the Gentile worlds, this is unlikely to be lasting or satisfactory.

6. Growing divergence between different cultures leads to a growing divergence in theology and practice. Time does not heal but exacerbate.[44]

7. Recrimination may eventually lead to mutual excommunication and the breaking of personal and official relations. Minds may be closed against each other for many generations.

Strand B is an important element

The part that is played by those who are both active in the new renewal movement and yet stay within the mainstream is of the greatest importance. In the Early Church the weakness and eventual disappearance of Strand B led to mutual hostility between Jews and Christians which has had appalling consequences for two thousand years and has weakened Christian theological development.

The desire for legitimation lowers boundaries

Any renewal finds an increasing desire to make itself more acceptable to the context in which it is set. Boundaries can be high at the beginning, but the need to live within the world means that they are reduced by time.[45] The early Gentile Church found itself accommodating to the Graeco-Roman world around it, and rejected those who tried to keep the boundaries high by an ascetic, world-denying stance. Paul steered the Church between the Charybdis of a new law (Col. 2:16–23) and the Scylla of moral licence: 'do not use your freedom as an opportunity for self-indulgence'.[46]

The world was not a place to be rejected with a shiver but to be gingerly accepted. Rulers were now to be prayed for; there were to be socially acceptable relationships between married couples, and between master and slave; laws were to be obeyed. The Christian faith, by virtue of the incarnation, has always taken the world seriously, and those who wished to withdraw from it were admired but not copied by many. The hermit and the ascetic have not been widely imitated, although their privations have often struck a chord in the Christian conscience when the Church has become too accommodating to the world.

There is a desire for authority within the renewal

As the close fellowship of the early disciples became more diffuse because of geography and numbers there became the need for a central authority. The apostles had a particular and unique authority and they were succeeded by elders, prophets and the self-appointed. Initially the leaders were church planters or wanderers moving from church to church, encouraging and disciplining. However, this became increasingly questionable and a more settled ministry of bishops became normal. Even this did not stop the search for authority and eventually super-bishops came into being with control over other bishops.

But bishops were not enough. In a Church beset by differing philosophies and outlooks it was inevitable that people should want a book which would give the ultimate answers. The canon of scripture quickly took shape, even if its final form eluded the Church for centuries.

The height of the boundary has to be adjusted

The boundary between faith and unfaith is crucial. In the early days of a renewal it is generally high, though in the infant Church it seems to have been fairly low, because of the remarkably good reception the Church had in Jerusalem. However, questions about the height of the boundary echo through the New Testament, with the Pauline letters arguing that it should not be too high.

A decision has to be made about the world outside the sect

The degree to which the height of the boundary has to be altered is largely dependent upon what is thought to be outside. If the non-sect world is believed to be like medieval maps, which declare of the unknown 'Here be dragons', then it will be regarded as hostile, totally corrupt and beyond redemption. As a result the boundary will be kept high. But if the world is reasonably friendly, manifestly good in parts and ripe for evangelism, the boundary will be lowered. When this is allied to the need for legitimation the general tendency of renewals is for boundaries to be lowered.

Renewals tend to lose force as they define themselves ever more closely

The move from the Greek-speaking to the Latin-speaking world had a profound effect on the Church. Verbal precision became essential to orthodoxy. The need for personal experience became less important, while mouthing the right form of words became vital. The Church looked inward as it tried to exclude the ideas it now counted as heresies, and evangelism became less instinctive. The way in which it handled Montanism showed a diminishing spiritual temperature and a distaste for the rough-and-ready. Christianity was becoming a sophisticated urban religion.

As we look at the process there is an air of inevitability about it. We are faced particularly acutely with the questions which this book seeks to address: 'How far is the change and apparent decline in renewals a natural part of human social behaviour?'; 'Is the Holy Spirit in this as much as in the original renewal?'; 'Is this intended by God so that the renewal can become part of the inheritance of the whole Church and not just a segment?'

Renewals are affected by social factors which are seldom recognised

The fact that Montanism came from a deeply unfashionable part of Asia Minor had a considerable effect on the way in which it was perceived, in the same way that Galilee was seen as less likely to produce a Messiah than Jerusalem. Archaeology has pointed out to us the considerable difference in lifestyle between the urban and the rural parts of the Roman Empire. The towns were impressive by any standards, with a cultured and comfortable way of life for a surprisingly high proportion of the people living in them. The rural areas, apart from the villas which had hardly begun to become common in the second century, were still seen as backward and conservative. The impressive civil engineering which made much of the urban lifestyle possible did not have much effect outside the city walls.

It is clear that the place a renewal comes from has a considerable effect upon its subsequent progress and how readily it is accepted by the mainstream.

The longer the time the greater the divergence

The history of the Ebionites and the Montanists well illustrates the growing incomprehension between those movements and the mainstream of the Church, and a steadily diverging theology and practice.

Truth tends to be defined by the intellect rather than by experience

The reliance on experience seen in the New Testament and in the Montanist movement in time gives way to a more intellectual approach to faith. Agreement to certain propositions is seen as at least as important as a personal encounter with God. In turn this can lead to a period of anti-intellectualism and dissatisfaction with their leadership among those who wish to affirm what they themselves have experienced and who become impatient of 'logic-chopping'. This is something encountered in some reactions to the modern ecumenical movement.

4   Renewal in the Cloister

We skip from the beginning of the first millennium to the end. The Church has moved from being a despised and persecuted minority to a position of power and prestige. The assertions made on its behalf have become more extreme. About AD 300 Cyprian had claimed 'extra ecclesiam nulla salus', with the implication that those who were adherents of the many heresies which swirled around the Church at the time were not saved by Christ. Later, despite the collapse of the Roman Empire, the Church survived to bring a measure of light. Indeed for Ireland and the areas around, the so-called Dark Ages were not dark, but a Golden Age to be looked back to as the time of the saints and of much beauty.

THE MONK SUCCEEDS THE MARTYR

It was a medieval commonplace, assumed but not examined, that the Apostles had been monks as they observed the idealised pattern described in Acts 2:42–47. After all, monks, like the Apostles, met to share the Eucharist, to eat and pray in fellowship together, to 'have all things in common'. Hence it was asserted that the monastic life was the only truly scripturally balanced life of work and prayer for a Christian. All others, it was implied, were second-class Christians.

Certainly the monks were the church planters, the people who prayed and the people who preached the gospel. After Constantine it was monasticism, begun in the East and expanding into the West, which led the way of mission. Augustine, Columba and the others who evangelised Anglo-Saxon

England were all monks. Others travelled deep into Eastern Europe and Russia with the gospel, while Nestorian monks reached India and China. By the end of the eighth century a network of monasteries brought prayer, education and a touch of the divine to a Europe recovering from the collapse of the Roman Empire and the tumult of many peoples on the move. At first there were many different rules by which monasteries were governed, but by the ninth century the common-sense spirituality of the Benedictine Rule was predominant.

In its early days monasticism was strongly missionary. The eighth-century Cambrai Homily referred to three kinds of martyrdom: white stood for an ascetic life; green for sorrow and penance; while red stood for total mortification for the sake of Christ in the service of others.[1] And this was not self-regarding, for early monks were convinced that they should not remain in their monastery seeking their own salvation but should serve and save others.

All was to end in chaos, however. By the end of the ninth century regular monastic observance had almost died out. Monasteries had become rich with many possessions and they also lay defenceless and helpless as easy pickings for any marauder. Frankia was devastated by undisciplined soldiers during the civil wars between the sons of Louis the Pious. The Vikings in their shallow-draughted boats struck far inland from the seaboard of the Baltic and the Atlantic and from any navigable river. The Saracens had occupied Sicily and attacked Italy, annihilating the greatest of monasteries at Monte Cassino. In 883 they burnt the foundation of St Benedict so completely that for sixty years it lay derelict. Only a handful of monastic houses survived, hidden by their remoteness from the disturbances – Fulda, Reichnau and St Gall were among them.

But the monastic movement did not falter just because of outside attacks. It had already withered from within. The growing riches and power of the Church meant that kings and nobles could not ignore so significant a part of the state. It became common for lay abbots to be appointed by monarchs and local landowners and the income diverted to their own treasuries. Often these lay abbots were of aristocratic blood, who in turn chose members of their own families to succeed them; frequently they had neither the spiritual nor the administrative capabilities required.[2] The lights were going out in the spiritual powerhouses even before the assaults of the Vikings and the Saracens.

CLUNY

Around AD 900, in this scene of devastation, a nineteen-year-old called Odo felt the call of God to enter a monastery. He lived at Tours, one of the great centres of monastic endeavour in the past. There was no monastery there now: he searched far around, but returned home disappointed. A more determined friend on the same quest found a surviving monastery at Baume. He returned to collect Odo and they became monks under Abbot Bruno who had restored the Rule of St Benedict of Aniane.[3] Shortly afterwards Duke William of Aquitaine decided to found a monastery on his estates. He sent for Bruno who found a suitable area and it was conveyed to the new foundation, including 'the serfs of both sexes'. The Foundation Charter of 910 starts in magnificent manner:

> To all right thinkers it is clear that the providence of God has so provided for certain rich men that, by means of their transitory possessions . . . they may be able to merit everlasting rewards . . . I, William, count and duke by grace of God, have considered it advisable . . . that I should give some little portion for the gain of my soul.

There then follow two passages, the terms of which restored the monastic life in Europe:

> those same monks shall have power and permission to elect any one of their order whom they please as abbot [without] the intervention of our own or any other power.

and:

those same monks, shall be subject neither to our yoke, nor that of our relatives, nor to the sway of the royal might, nor to that of any earthly power.

Cluny was to have the right to order its own affairs, and was answerable only to the Pope.[4]

Bruno was the first abbot and he was followed by 'four spiritual leaders of genius, each of which in their own way stamped his imprint not only on the regime of Cluny but upon the religious life of his age'.[5] The Benedictine pattern that they followed was one in which the 'voice of prayer was never silent'. Otherwise there was a profound silence which was perceived as participating in the eternal silence of God himself. Wherever they were they were supposed to focus on God, so that even when travelling they recited psalms to themselves. The intention was a severe simplicity of behaviour, of surroundings and of spiritual life.

Among the privations of ordinary life and the threats of political intrigue a Cluniac community must have seemed an oasis of wholesomeness. Their success was immediate and their reputation exploded. Only a few years after the community's foundation monks from Cluny were being asked to lead reforms in other areas, including Rome itself. As the years passed they spread vastly until by the time of St Hugh there were over one thousand Cluniac monasteries.[6] So many wanted to join that numbers in each monastery had to be limited – Cluny allowed a maximum of 300. Each dependent monastery had their abbot appointed by Cluny and every one of their monks was in theory a monk of the community at Cluny itself. It was 'a ramshackle spiritual empire' but it affected vast numbers for its influence led to many other reforms in the Church as a whole which quickened its spiritual bloodstream.

But after the reform came the gradual relapse. Wealth flowed towards an organisation which had such a considerable influence, as each dependent monastery paid a small tax to Cluny in return for their support. Eventually it seemed to mirror the feudal overlordship which was the current secular form of government.

Worship was their raison d'être so the Cluniacs began to build impressive buildings to the glory of God in which to praise him more splendidly. In its day the church at Cluny was, at 555 feet long, the largest in Christendom. Odilo exulted that he 'had found it wood and was leaving it marble'. Public prayer was the heart of their life but it began to take up such a large proportion of time that it crowded out the manual work which was part of the Benedictine ideal. Further, the worship became so splendid and elaborate that it absorbed all their resources of time and energy.

Finally, despite its income, Cluny got into debt. Unseen at the time, but probably the main reason was the gradual inflation which Europe experienced during the eleventh century. More obvious and less insidious were the effects of the social services which the monasteries provided in their neighbourhoods, for their pastoral care was often impressive. More sapping were the 'corrodies'. Initially these were pensions given to the poor but it did not take long for the aristocracy to realise that this was a cheap way to offload their old retainers. The cost to the monasteries was great.

The sparkling spiritual renewal of the tenth century had become the overweight leviathan of the twelfth. Up to eight hours a day in liturgical worship gave little time for personal communion with God, nor for physical work, nor for care of those around: the primitive Benedictine idea of a balance of prayer, manual work and study had become distressingly lopsided. The monasteries' buildings, once so rudimentary that Odo had to apologise for them, had soared expensively upwards. The early simplicity was overtaken by the complexities of running an ecclesiastical empire. As considerable landowners, they had feudal obligations to the king: they had to hold courts, collect taxes and even raise armies.[7] Their leaders walked with kings and emperors[8] – who often used the monasteries' commodious buildings as stopping places for themselves and their myriad of hangers-on. Debts multiplied. Lay stewards were appointed to manage the estates but it made little difference. The reform itself was in desperate need of reform.

Criticism

Grievances mounted. In particular St Bernard put forward a series of robust but reasoned arguments, which his friend Abbot Peter the Venerable sought to answer, none too successfully, on behalf of Cluny. Bernard claimed that the vow of 'poverty' meant little when, despite having given up their personal possessions, the monks lived in great buildings, wore fine clothes and ate well. They were looked after for life; few outside the monastery walls had this level of security. He complained of the ornate stone carvings in their churches, which still intrigue us:

> In the sight of the brethren reading in the cloister, what is that ridiculous monstrosity doing? what is that deformed beauty and that beautiful deformity? those unclean monkeys? those ferocious lions? those battling knights . . . on all sides one sees such a rich and amazing variety of forms that it is more pleasing to read the marbles than the manuscripts.

The precision and splendour of their liturgy no longer reflected the wonder of the worship of heaven but had become an end in itself. Further, Bernard objected to their possessions: 'Towns, villas, serfs, servants and handmaidens, and, what is worse, the gain arising from toll duties . . .'⁹ Apostolic poverty had given way to riches, communion with God to formalised ceremonial, simplicity of soul to complexity of administration, manual work to the token pulling up of a weed.

One curious incident brought much to a head. After the death of Hugh, Pons was elected as abbot. After some years he resigned his abbacy in order to go on pilgrimage to the Holy Land and Peter was elected in his place. Three years later Pons returned and tried to take back the abbacy by force. He and some discontented monks stormed the abbey and sacked it.

Eventually the secular authorities had to be called in and Pons died in the dungeons of the Pope in Rome in 1126. It did the reputation of Cluny no good at all. Abbot Peter tried to reform Cluny itself and restore a greater discipline and simpler life-style. But the attempt came to nothing, largely because the monks refused to accept the changes. As a result it remained a diminishing force in Christendom for many years, though its great buildings still stand as a reminder of its eminence.

The reform of the reform

The reforms which sprang from the decay of Cluny were immensely fruitful. They took at least five main directions: some wanted a more personal God; some wanted to evangelise the world for Christ; some wanted a deeper study of the ways of God; some wanted to take up arms for Christ; some wanted to be monks while doing the ordinary work of a parish priest. It is an intriguing time, for from the dying of Cluny came a fountain of new ideas and ideals – in many ways reflecting the overall vigour and prosperity of twelfth-century Europe. Unfortunately we can only sketch it out for the purposes of this book for it is the growth and decline of Cluny which is our main concern.

There were many in the monasteries who wanted just to be with God and to get away from the tedious liturgical trappings and ecclesiastical politics. They wanted a return to the simplicity of the original vision of St Benedict. In other words, they wanted to return to the ideal of Cluny before it had become encrusted with impedimenta. Bernard himself trod this path and founded the monastery of Clairvaux which was to become the headquarters of the Cistercian order.

Others wanted an even more austere regime and wanted to be hermits, hoping thereby to rekindle the holiness of the Desert Fathers. Like the third-century hermits in the Syrian desert, they eventually gathered together and the Carthusians were formed in the bleakest surroundings that could be found.[10] Each monk lived in his own cell, sharing only vespers each day with his brothers; the eucharist was celebrated together only on Sundays and Holy Days. They ate alone and generally prayed separately, for their lives were given to contemplation of the being of the living God. Lay brothers did the inevitable business of the community.[11]

The hermits fled from the world; the friars threw themselves at it. They saw the growing urban centres largely neglected by the Church and determined to take the gospel to them. The Franciscans and the Dominicans were mobile, unencumbered preachers. They begged their way from place to place, their only possessions the clothes they stood up in. Their way of life can have been barely distinguishable from the wild-eyed beggars and the mountebanks who inhabited the towns of North Italy and France. Inevitably they clashed with local clergy and bishops, but they were directly responsible to the Pope, and did not fear the interference of local ecclesiastics.

The Dominicans were not only preachers, but in the course of time developed into scholars. In a period when many intellectual seeds were germinating, they saw the need for part of the evangelistic work of the Church to be to speak the truth in the marketplace of competing ideas. They began work in the infant universities of Europe and soon had a formidable academic reputation.

During the eleventh and twelfth centuries Europe was under pressure from outside. The Vikings were a waning power, though the conquest of Britain can be seen as their last and greatest success, for William the Conqueror was of Viking stock. Muslims had overrun the eastern borders of Byzantium after the battle of Manzikert in 1071 and were pressing up through Spain. They were intent on extending an area which stretched from the Atlantic almost to the borders of China in which there was a common faith, a common coinage, a common language and a civilisation that was in advance of Christian Europe. Their earlier tolerance of Christians changed when the Seljuk Turks occupied Syria and Palestine, subjecting the Christian inhabitants to appalling persecution and attacking those on pilgrimage to Jerusalem. Later still, the Mongols of frightful reputation broke into the Muslim civilisation (though in the process becoming Muslims themselves). They penetrated terrifyingly far into Austria, Poland and Hungary and menaced the whole of Europe.

The monastic movement took a strange turn when monks began to take up the sword for Christ. The crusades began in 1095 and spawned the Military Orders of the Hospitallers and the Templars. Following the monastic model, the knights took vows and attempted to keep a simplified monastic lifestyle in defence of *Outremer* – the Christian enclave in the Holy Land. In the Slavic lands overrun by Islam, the Knights of the Teutonic Order and the Knights of the Sword fought for generations, propelling Lithuania into a short-lived kingdom which stretched from the Baltic to the Black Sea.

Alongside these exotic blooms the quiet desire of ordinary clergy to lead a more consecrated life through a form of monasticism adapted to parochial ministry seems mundane in the extreme. However, in the cathedrals and major town churches there was a move towards the clergy becoming 'canons regular'. They lived as far as possible a communal life, observing monastic worship and taking the threefold vow of poverty, celibacy and obedience. Most adopted the so-called Rule of St Augustine. This was based on a letter sent by Augustine to his sister when she entered a religious community, but spruced up for practical use six hundred years later. The Augustinians became a powerful force for the growth of spiritual life in ordinary churches for many years.

THE HYPOTHESIS

In contrast with the Early Church where Strand A came to dominate, the reform of the monasteries is of particular interest because it is a reform which is kept entirely within Strand B. The Cluniac monasteries persevered within the Church; indeed they were often commended by popes against attacks from bishops and powerful lay people.

Stage 1: Renewal

The romantic tale of the foundation of Cluny begins with William of Aquitaine asking Bruno to choose a site and then being irked because the latter picked some of his best hunting grounds. After the miseries of the eighth and ninth centuries there was a longing by many to find God in a personal and real way and it expressed itself in the only way they knew: the pattern they chose was the one which had been successful in earlier times – the monastic life. Cluny was one of the first and certainly the most influential, but there were similar stirrings in other places, in particular at Gorze in Lorraine and at Brogne in Flanders. They began independently though all looked back to the inheritance of St Benedict.

The monastic renewal was to have a massive impact on the Church and even on international politics for many decades. Its effect was to make God more central in the violent and disturbed society which was contemporary Europe.

Stage 2: Conflict

The ready acceptance of the leaders of Cluny by popes and kings should not hide the fact that they were bitterly resented by many ordinary bishops and clergy, for the Cluniacs by their very presence and enthusiasm were clearly, at least in their early years, a condemnation of the spiritual and educational inadequacies of the clergy. Even worse, they claimed to be the only Christians living a truly apostolic life, relegating others to second-class status. And even more galling for Church leaders must have been the fact that the Cluniacs had easy access to Rome and that the Pope used them as spiritual shock troops to bring reform and discipline to other places, whether they wanted it or not.[12]

It was not just clerics who were upset. The wise safeguards of Duke William meant the monks were free of interference in their affairs by secular authorities in their locality. Resentment festered, and in later years when the monasteries became rich and powerful they were inevitably the target of envy and animosity: here was an important element in the state which it was difficult to control, even if the monasteries did have to fulfil their feudal duties.

When the later abbots of Cluny became involved in the political controversies of their time they inevitably made more enemies. Hugh in particular, with his noble birth and his leadership of the Cluniac monasteries when they were at their most influential, was caught up in the long-drawn 'investiture controversy'. The details do not concern us, but it began as a challenge by Pope Gregory VII to the emperor and virtually all the kings of Europe. Previously these had claimed the right to invest new bishops with the symbols of their office – their ring and crosier. Along with this came an acknowledgement by the bishops of their acceptance of the feudal authority of the monarch. The quarrel rumbled on for half a century and led to the creation of the anti-pope Clement III, the excommunication of large numbers of people and, eventually, the complete victory of the papacy. Hugh, as a fervent supporter of Rome, antagonised many secular authorities.

Stage 3: Networking

The Cluniac reform was almost too successful in its networking. From the first the monasteries realised they had to communicate with each other if their movement was to be cohesive and effective. The reality was daunting. The abbots of Cluny were faced with the problem of how to keep some control over many hundreds of monasteries scattered throughout the romance-speaking areas of Europe. As a result all the abbots travelled extensively. This was a spiritual duty, for the abbot was regarded as the spiritual father of every single Cluniac monk. This meant, even more unrealistically, that all novices in all the monasteries had to make their profession directly to the abbot of Cluny, so they had either to travel to Cluny or to wait until he visited their monastery. Southern Europe was crisscrossed by abbots of dependent monasteries making their way to Cluny to receive advice and spiritual help and to deal with the matters of finance and discipline which took an increasing amount of their time. The expenditure of time, especially by the senior people in the monastery, was prodigious.

Within the context of the communications system of medieval Europe it was the best that could be managed, but the practical problems of networking a thousand monasteries up to a thousand miles apart were never solved.

Stage 4: Definition

In a Strand B renewal, definition in terms of doctrine is less important than for those in Strand A. Renewals which break away from the mainstream have to define themselves over against the rest of the Church in order to provide a rationale for their existence. This is a less insistent necessity for those in Strand B. The Cluniac reform never needed to do this, especially as they were returning to an old tradition – a fresh renaissance of the Rule of St Benedict.

But definition also means institutionalisation. The organisation grows and becomes bureaucratic. Its boundaries have to be defined. Cluny had no difficulty in defining who were its monks and who were not, but the position of others in its monasteries was always difficult. The problem stemmed from the time when Duke William handed over the 'serfs, servants and handmaids' for the service of the monastery. Even the ascetic Carthusians found it necessary to have lay people to run their business affairs. Far, far more were needed for the great tracts of land and business interests that Cluny came to enjoy. How were these necessary but difficult to define people to be treated? Were they within or outside the monastic community?

The Cluniac monasteries evolved a formidable bureaucratic structure, run mainly by lay people. However, it became necessary to allow some monks to be excused the long periods of worship in order to attend to the demands of their great estates and the negotiations which were required with local and national authorities. It did their spiritual lives no good.

The other boundary area was the engagement of the monastery in the world outside. The ground of so much of
the criticism of Cluny focused on this – they were too much
at home in the world, too little retired from it. The space
and peace had gone, subsumed in a forest of activities. Some
of these activities were socially beneficial, but much time
was spent simply servicing the extravagant needs of the
organisation itself.

Stage 5: Divergence

In the overall plan divergence is the stage when the renewal
itself is divided into those who leave the mainstream and those
who stay inside. In a primarily Strand B renewal, such as we
are considering, this does not happen. At a late stage, as
we have seen, there was a flowering of many offshoots, but all
remained within the mainstream Church.

Stage 6: Communication

As a Strand B renewal the community of Cluny was able to
keep in touch with the mainstream of the Church and was
therefore able to communicate more easily the joy of what
was happening. Communication was by the only means available to them – personal contact after many miles of weary
travelling, and letters which had themselves to be carried by
hand.

The significance of this reform was very quickly recognised,
and the Cluniacs were thereafter used by popes to invigorate
spiritual life in many places which needed an injection of real
faith, even in Rome itself.

Stage 7: Consequences

After the decline of Cluny there were two principal results.
First, Cluny itself was assimilated (Stage 7c). The main stem
which grew straight from the original foundation remained for

many years, but its former glory had long since departed. It merely became one amongst a host of different religious orders. The monastery at Cluny itself was closed in 1790: the final coda on an extraordinary history.

But this prolonged death was far from being the full story. The Cluniac reform also led to Stage 7a, where fragmentation takes place. For a Strand A movement this is nearly always fatal as it splinters into smaller and smaller sects. If Cluny is a true guide, a Strand B renewal can have more fruitful consequences for the Church, for from the movement's own reform can come good for the whole.

The number of different directions that new reform movements took when Cluny ran to seed in the twelfth century is startling. Many of the religious orders we have today had their genesis in the reaction against Cluny. It was as if the river of spiritual vitality which had flowed from Cluny for so long had now branched out into many different streams. And along the banks of the streams there was much good fruit – with the possible exception of the military orders!

CONCLUSIONS

The Cluniac reform is a fine example of a Strand B renewal. There was never any question of the renewal movement leaving the mainstream Church and it had a manifest impact on the whole Church. Even its decay helped the Church in that it led to the introduction of new experiments. The fruit of Cluny remains with us.

Strand B needs fewer people to start a renewal than Strand A

The early history of Cluny is dominated by a very few individuals – Bruno, Odo and a handful of early followers. A renewal within the mainstream needs only a few initiators to have a considerable influence. If someone leaves the mainstream, however, he or she needs to be part of a sizeable group if they are to have the critical mass needed to establish the renewal. The individual needs support to be able to sustain a Strand A renewal. A church of one will not succeed: it will be stillborn and disappear.

Moreover, a Strand A renewal has to grow quickly if it is to establish itself. Without expansion it can all too easily become a dwindling band destined for extinction. Such rapid growth is not so necessary for a Strand B renewal, where a prophet can speak for many years before being heard.[13]

Possessions choke renewals

The Cluniac reforms began to decay when the monasteries started to accumulate things. It was difficult for them to avoid doing so. People, including many who were influential, were so grateful for what the Cluniacs had done that they showered wealth on them. Gifts of land and money flowed towards them.

With possessions came complexity. The estates that the monasteries were given were not just open fields. They came complete with what was on them: villages and mills and roads, and also the people who worked the fields and ground the corn and used the roads. The Cluniacs also gained the feudal duties attached to the land, with the obligations and the local politics which that entailed. What seemed to be a result of the growth and flourishing of the renewal in fact ate out its heart.

The routinisation of charisma may be inevitable as a movement grows but the process is speeded up by the acquiring of property; we may not have feudal duties demanded by our lord, but all property involves responsibilities and taxes and anxiety.[14] Nowhere is this seen more clearly than in church buildings. For Cluny it was a temptation that was not resisted for they built in order to house the splendid worship which was offered to God. It meant that the monastic house came to be associated with excessively ornate buildings and grandeur of architecture. In this they were following current fashion, for this was the great age of cathedral building in Europe – Chartres from 1130, Durham from 1093, Westminster Abbey from the tenth century onwards. Cluny both helped to begin and also aped this development.

The institutionalisation of their movement was all too obvious to many at Cluny for they knew they were being choked to death but felt powerless to prevent it. When Peter the Venerable debated with St Bernard there is a note of apology which shows that he had more than a little sympathy with the points that Bernard was raising but felt duty bound to defend the organisation of which he was abbot. Further, he knew all too well that he was a spokesperson for a community which had all too many monks who liked the comfortable life and the security which a prosperous monastery could bring. His own efforts at reform could not but be a compromise, for the leader of a divided organisation is bound by the 'art of the possible'.

Renewal, like any human endeavour, has its own momentum, and those involved, although they may well know that things are going wrong, yet feel incapable of stopping the slide towards decay and disillusionment. Often it is the leaders who have the overall view and are therefore most aware of this, and also of their own helplessness in being able to stop what is happening. Denominations today may experience this dilemma: leaders are conscious of weakening, and there are many who suggest solutions, but the right path to take and the courage to follow it is not given to many trapped within the system. Like Peter the Venerable, the best that such leaders can hope for is a moderate reform within the existing structure, though that is no easy matter in itself.

The renewal needed renewal. Cluny can be said to represent all those renewal movements within the Church which have become moribund. One solution is that adopted by Bernard – to break away and begin a new renewal. But that renewal will itself soon be in need of renewal. As Visser d'Hooft said, renewal leads 'a precarious existence'. But that is its strength – the need for reliance upon God and the knowledge of the reality of human nature. To forget the first is to betray the renewal; to forget the second is to invite despair.

The greatest strengths can become the greatest weaknesses

The renewal of worship in Cluny was wonderful indeed. Initially their worship was heartfelt, joyful and real; but it became complex, hidebound and lifeless. Above all, it came to sprawl so unmanageably that it crowded out the balanced life that St Benedict had advocated in his Rule.

Renewals are always in danger of making their greatest asset their greatest handicap. What makes them different and special needs to be emphasised, but if it is not kept in check it will inevitably come to be the only thing on offer. Not all renewals have to do with the monastic life, and therefore do not all have the wisdom of St Benedict to guide them. Balance must be kept. The temptation is often to over-emphasise one element and in doing so to fall into error. 'The Devil's Distortion' points out the danger to the Church of allowing:

> authority to become authoritarianism
> sacraments to be regarded as magic
> love of Scripture to become bibliolatry
> every member ministry to descend into anarchy
> individual insight to become individualism
> differing gifts to produce fragmentation
> freedom to allow licence
> expressions of emotion to become emotionalism
> statements of opinion to distort into manipulation
>
> – and driving central truths to the fringe
> and secondary matters to the centre[15]

Intellectually it is dangerous and emotionally it is unhealthy to allow one element of the faith to dominate. This is as true of an individual, a local church, a denomination or the whole Church of Christ. In history a full-orbed Trinitarian faith has been found to be the best antidote.

Growth can breed fantasy

Cluny became an empire with thousands of monks, tens of thousands of people dependent upon them and possessions which kings envied. But it became overwhelmed by numbers. It lost its spiritual cutting edge, became institutionalised and bureaucratised, and absorbed in the administrative load that ensued. Cluny, like many another renewal at both local and wider level, found it hard to cope with either God or Mammon and ended by falling between the two – neither a powerful spiritual dynamo nor a successful secular organisation.

Like many another renewal, it tried to manage the spiritual problem by resorting to fantasy. The fiction that the Abbot of Cluny could in reality be the spiritual Father of every Cluniac monk and the head of every Cluniac monastery was nonsensical. Unfortunately this assumption of pastoral care is common when a church grows, when a renewal becomes widespread or an organisation increases. Pastors of churches with hundreds of people are supposed to know the personal details of all, bishops are supposed to be 'Fathers in God' to all in their dioceses, organisations are supposed to be able to deal with every crisis. This is not confined to the Church. Social services are supposed to cope with every personal problem, the police with every crime, the government with every ill.

The problems of growth are insidious because they manifest themselves gradually. More than that, growth is rightly seen as a source of joy rather than concern. Therefore the questions are not asked and none of the necessary steps which are required are put in place.

Renewals can be self-deluding, those involved supposing that the cohesion and sense of common purpose which were so exhilarating in the early days would continue when numbers multiply. A cell of twenty is not different from a congregation of two hundred or two thousand merely because of numbers but because of its character as a human organism. The larger has inevitably to be more remote and more bureaucratic if it is to function satisfactorily. The leader is less available – a bishop or superintendent caring for two hundred churches cannot, with the best will in the world, be as accessible as someone caring for a handful. Yet the myth remains. It is devastating to churches because it leads to the frustration of expectations which can never be met. Even more destructive is the effect upon leaders because of the competing tensions they endure and the inner guilt which comes from knowing that they will never satisfy the expectations.

The communal swamps the individual

Cluny began as a group of people seeking God: it drew Odo and his friend across Frankia till they discovered the monastery of Bruno. They found that their spiritual lives drew strength from the common life. Sadly, and typically, the movement they founded ended by denying the very same needs they had sought themselves. They had wanted to be alone with God, to learn about him, to 'practise the Presence'. St Benedict had wanted communal worship, but also time for meditation and study alone with God. The Cluniac practice as it developed crowded out time for study and private prayer. It became too easy for the Cluniac monk to rely upon the spiritual life of his fellow rather than his own life with the Lord.

The same can be seen in other renewals. Excitement is generated in the big meeting or the great conference, new ideas are found in the interchange of fellowship meetings, corporate prayer of such vitality is novel. But the reality of spiritual renewal is ultimately the aloneness of each person with the Lord their God. There has to be space – and Cluny forgot this. Many of the movements which grew out of Cluny, in reaction against its togetherness, emphasised the need for personal study and prayer. The austerity of the Carthusian in his cell could hardly point the contrast more vividly.

The result of an over-emphasis on the communal can mean that the renewal comes to be seen, not in personal spiritual growth, but in the culture with which the renewal is surrounded. For Cluny that environment was the glory of worship:

there must have been many monks and an even greater proportion of visitors who thought that worship in the Cluniac
style *was* the Cluniac renewal. There were many Americans
who saw the camp meeting as the essential element in their
Revivals, just as in modern times charismatic choruses or Cursillo weekends have been seen as being pivotal when they are
in fact peripheral and only the means to an end – as well as
being good examples of 'driving central truths to the fringe and
secondary matters to the centre'.

Spiritual elitism flourishes

Inevitably if some are seen as spiritual giants it makes others
look like spiritual pygmies. The monastic movement by its very
nature cannot but give this impression. Here are people who
have taken vows of poverty, chastity and obedience, while
others have not experienced this public renunciation. Their very
presence can be seen as a reproach to the half-heartedness of
the rest of us. Needless to say, that is not what is intended but
that can be the perception gained by others.

Any renewal incurs this risk. If the people who are involved
are the same as everyone else there is no sense in which their
life has been turned upside down by God. Jesus said 'by
their fruits you shall know them' and while others may rejoice
in those fruits, the reality is that their presence is itself a
challenge which is not always faced.

Those who are outside a renewal can deal with its claims in
one of three ways.

1. They can deny the reality of what they see. Changed lives
   can be brushed aside and practical outworkings of a
   renewal dismissed. The monks of Cluny had to put up with
   considerable mockery (as had the Montanists before them).
2. They can denigrate the people concerned. Remarks such as
   'It will not last', 'Pride comes before a fall' and similar
   expressions may be used. This is heightened if there is a
   lapse on the part of someone involved, especially if they

are in a position of leadership. Thus the abbots of Cluny, who we now see as remarkable men, were in their day heartily disliked by many ecclesiastics as well as some secular authorities. The curious episode concerning ex-abbot Pons was seized upon to make Cluny the laughing stock of Europe.

3. They can deny its message. This may involve rejecting the theological stance of the renewal, denigrating the teaching abilities of its leaders, or being unwilling to consider the intellectual or spiritual challenge it poses. Cluny had to face a barrage of biblical texts which were thrown like missiles. Just like many subsequent renewals, they had to confront a logic-chopping examination of the Scriptures, instigated not in order to discover truth but to deny it. There are too many Christian Sadducees who 'know neither the Scriptures nor the power of God'.[16]

Decay into Life

It is difficult to think of any renewal which was as productive as Cluny in its decline. The new shoots put out from the fallen trunk are outlined above – the contemplative orders, the clergy in community, the military orders, the scholars and the friars. All lasted for centuries, many to the present day, though the successors of the crusaders have had to change their purpose!

The renewal of renewal movements is dependent upon certain factors, which we can trace in the story of Cluny.

1. Being a Strand B renewal Cluny was in contact with the mainstream of the Church. It was therefore able to influence the Church for good during its early life and its decline became a matter of concern throughout the Church. There were some small Strand A reform movements which sprang up outside the mainstream but had little positive effect and soon perished – often, like the Waldensians and the Cathars, under harsh persecution.

2. The Benedictine inspiration which led to the founding of

Cluny had not been forgotten. Many, like Bernard, were trying to reclaim what had been lost. If a dying renewal can leave behind it the memory of the original vision there will often be those who will pick up the discarded torch and run with it.

3. If Cluny had not declined would the new forms of life have appeared? This is an impossible question, but it is certainly arguable that in the overall purposes of God it was necessary. Possibly the epitaph of Cluny might be:

Unless a grain of wheat falls into the earth and dies,
it remains just a single grain;
but if it dies it bears much fruit.[17]

5 Renewal in the Church

The Reformation is far too large a subject to deal with in a book of this size, and it would be wearisome to examine the hypothesis in the same detail as previously. For our purposes the Reformation can teach us three things.

First, we can see that the first four parts of the hypothesis can be traced with ease through this period of Church history. The initial *renewal* stemmed from both an intellectual maelstrom and also a longing among many for a more God-centred and a less Church-controlled faith. This led to a period of *conflict* which lasted for much of the sixteenth century and, linked to political ambition, for many bloody years thereafter. *Networking* began early in the Reformation as its leaders wrote voluminously to each other and met frequently. The time of *definition* came almost simultaneously and led to the writings of Luther and Calvin and many others, through which there was a complete recasting of the Christian faith, not merely a defining of matters of dispute.[1]

Secondly, the Reformation is an example of a renewal which *diverged*, took all too long to *communicate* and whose *consequences* are a matter of serious debate today.

Thirdly, it gives us fascinating insights into the implications of renewal for the mission of the Church. It is often assumed that the renewal of a church at local or national level automatically leads to an emphasis on mission. The story of the Reformation questions this supposition.

REFORMATION AND COUNTER REFORMATION

Charles Williams characteristically set the scene with a touch of poetry:

> The Middle Ages did not know that they were ending but they did know that they were changing. They knew that the East had fallen and that the Turk, that Islam and its Unincarnate Deity, were in Constantinople, and threatening the West. They knew also that Antiquity had returned – in manuscripts, in statues, in prestige. They knew that navigation was expanding . . . they were the heirs of everything. Over all Europe there went up a kind of scream of colour.[2]

The 'scream of colour' was heard by scholars and saints, by kings and peasants. The rainbow began to play around the individual human being, rather than God Almighty. People were far from being irreligious but there was a burst of life which sought to be free of the confines of feudalism and the Church. In fifteenth-century Italy the outburst of vigour we call the Renaissance had begun and inflamed the rest of Europe. The human being became the hub of the intellectual universe at the same time as others were questioning whether the earth was the centre of the physical universe. The *uome universale* was the complete human being – someone at home in the arts, in science, in philosophy, in sport and in love. Tne accomplishments of a few still leave us marvelling: from its dawn in Dante to the poetry of Shakespeare via the masterpieces of Michelangelo and Leonardo, the Renaissance produced an age of the extraordinary.

Shakespeare describes through the voice of Hamlet the Renaissance wonder at the potential of a human being:

> What a piece of work is a man!
> How noble in reason! how infinite in faculty!
> In form, in moving, how express and admirable!
> In action how like an angel! in apprehension how like a
> god!

All things were debated and religious matters more than most. It is not surprising that the reaction against this free thinking gained strength. The Inquisition had been founded in 1233 as part of the campaign against the Albigenses (a heretic sect in southern France), but it was in the fifteenth and sixteenth centuries that it had its full impact: in Spain alone 60,000 cases were tried.[3] In 1557 the Vatican published the first Index Librorum Prohibitorum in a desperate attempt to curtail the new thinking, evidence of which was pouring off the newly invented printing presses.[4]

Many causes have been put forward for the Reformation. Some have given sociological explanations: 'whenever Christianity has become the religion of the fortunate and cultured and has grown philosophical, abstract, formal and ethically harmless in the process, the lower strata of society find themselves religiously expatriated'.[5] Others look to the reaction against the aggrandisement of power by the papacy. Cyprian's statement *extra ecclesiam nulla salus* had, through Unam Sanctam in 1302, become 'we declare, state, define, and proclaim that it is altogether necessary to salvation for every human creature to be subject to the Roman pontiff'.[6] Salvation did not come from being part of the fellowship of the Church but in being in obedience to the Pope. This doctrine was not without critics. The Conciliarists[7] held that a General Council of the Church was supreme, but they had wilted in the face of the refusal by the medieval popes to allow for anybody superior to themselves.

Scientific ideas were challenging the God-centred universe. In medieval times the interior of the human body was seen as sacrosanct, but anatomists had begun to discover how it worked. However, the power of the Church was still great. Leonardo hid his fine drawings during his lifetime. Copernicus resurrected the theory of the sun-centred planetary system that Aristarchus has suggested in 250 BC. He too was cautious, only publishing his ideas on his death-bed.[8]

The rediscovery of classical literature introduced Europe to the pagan world of Olympus, and it revealed that different religious beliefs had been held by philosophers like Socrates and Plato whom people had come to revere. The world of thought was not entirely Christian.

Out of this welter of differences there grew the Reformation. It was led by an elite, people with their own passionate agendas, who pushed forward the questions which were to prove so explosive.[9] That the Church needed reform was obvious to all except the extreme conservatives: in Spain reforms were being introduced forty years before Luther nailed his theses to the door of Wittenburg church in 1517. How was it to be done? Was it to be a reform of the structure and practice of the Church by edict from the Pope, or was it to be through a General Council of the Church, or should individual dioceses reform themselves? But others wanted to go further. Ideas sparkled. Some wanted a complete rebuilding of the whole ark of the Christian faith. Others, like Luther, Calvin and the English reformers, just wanted to knock off what they regarded as the doctrinal barnacles which had attached themselves over the years and which hid the simplicity of the faith of Christ. Luther's 95 theses criticised the practice of indulgences, which he saw as just such a theological accretion as well as being financially suspect.

Divergence (Stage 5)

The stage was set for one of the greatest and most painful divergences in Christian history. The anathemas hurled by Pope and Patriarch at each other centuries before when the Eastern and Western Churches parted had hurt few. But the Reformation set country against country, town against town, neighbour against neighbour, one member of a family against another. The line between Catholic and Protestant states came to lie across Europe like a sixteenth-century Berlin Wall, with bitter conflicts over disputed territory.

There were two Reformations: one resulted in the new churches of the Reformation, the second reformed the Catholic Church from within. In the language of our hypothesis, Strand

A represents the Protestants and Strand B the Counter Reformation.

At the end of the fifteenth century few except the extreme conservatives did not realise that something had to be done about the clergy. While there were more good priests and bishops than is sometimes supposed, there were too many who were idle, drunken, promiscuous and vicious. Professor Owen Chadwick says:

> If we seek a single theme running through the reforming endeavours of the Catholic reformation, it would be quest for more adequate clergy – better-trained, and better-instructed priests, priests resident in their parishes, bishops resident in their sees, pastors fervent and self-sacrificing and missionary-minded, trained as confessors, celibate, mortified, able to teach in school, wearing canonical dress; a priesthood uncorrupted and incorruptible, educated and other-worldly.[10]

Nor was it merely the parish priests who needed to be reformed. Many monasteries had declined from their high ideals to become intensely reactionary and hostile to any true spirituality. St John of the Cross and St Teresa both encountered strong opposition to their reforms. St John endured nine months of cruel imprisonment in a Carmelite monastery. It was not only Henry VIII who closed monasteries and appropriated their possessions: in the name of reform Cardinal Ximenes had been doing the same in Spain years before Henry and Thomas Cromwell began their work. As Bonomi said, 'The best way to fight the heretics is not to deserve their criticism'.

Many felt that the old monastic orders were beyond redemption. Instead they founded new ones: the 1520s and 1530s saw the foundation of the Theatines, the Somaschi, the Barnabites and, above all, the Jesuits. Reform was happening fast from the Catholic side as well as among the early Protestants.

A possible way out of the growing crisis was the idea that there should be a General Council of the Church which would reform it from within. Luther and many of the other Reformers looked to this as a possible solution which could maintain the unity of the Church. But the popes at first refused to entertain the idea, remembering the challenges to papal authority which had come from the earlier Councils of Constance (1414–18) and Basle (1431–49). However the accession of Paul III in 1534 made reform possible. He commissioned a group of nine reformers to prepare a 'Report of a Select Committee on Reforming the Church': they produced a blistering condemnation of much of its life. The report was kept secret but, as is normal in such matters, it leaked. It led in turn to the theological Colloquy of Ratisbon in 1541 between moderate Reformers and moderate Catholics, probably the last chance to retain unity. The Colloquy reached remarkable agreement under the leadership of Cardinal Contarini but, unfortunately, as has happened in recent discussions between Anglicans and Roman Catholics, moderate theologians do not always recognise that they are not fully representative. Conservative Catholics and many Reformers, including Luther, refused to accept Ratisbon.

It was not until 1545 that the long-awaited Council took place at the small town of Trent. While the Pope never attended a session in person, papal influence was evident through his nuncios who directed and controlled proceedings. The Council went on intermittently until 1563. Its dealing with disciplinary matters led to a tightening of authority and greater control over the clergy. Indeed, possibly the greatest long-term effect was the requirement that all clergy should be educated at a diocesan seminary. Though this took many years to put into effect it eventually removed many of the scandals of ignorance and loose living which had been so damaging.

It was unlikely that Trent could ever have brought Protestants and Catholics together. It was not until 1551, six years after it started, that Protestant representatives were eventually allowed to come to the Council, and by that time the doctrinal statements, nearly all of them strongly anti-Protestant in tone, were already in place. Moreover, during these years the conservative wing of the Catholics was becoming more powerful. From 1542 onwards the Inquisition was allowed to hold special papal courts in Italy and thereby began a witch hunt in which not only Protestantism but much that was artistic and civilised was suppressed. Even cardinals were not safe from its reach for, as Cardinal Caraffa, the Inquisitor General, said, 'on their punishment, the salvation of the classes beneath them depends'. Pope Paul IV (1555–59) had a violent dislike of Protestants and an even greater hatred of the Spanish, which led to some curious situations in which he employed Protestants to fight Spaniards in the Low Countries and reproached Queen Mary of England, despite her Catholic zeal, for supporting the Spanish.[11]

The Counter Reformation was in full swing – conservative and energetic in tone, it had a deep spirituality and an authoritarian stance. Trent had set the tone for the next four centuries.

MISSION IN REFORMATION AND COUNTER REFORMATION

Nowhere is the activist nature of the Counter Reformation seen more than in its mission. There was an outburst of educational work throughout Catholic Europe, largely under the leadership of the new religious orders. There were also attempts to win back the areas lost to the 'heretics'. The responsibility for this was firmly in the hands of the Pope, who sent missionary bishops ('vicars apostolic') into such countries.

There was also a growth of missionary work outside Europe. Since South and Central America were perceived as being Catholic through the conquests of the Spanish and the Portuguese, they became the earliest stage for their enthusiasm. At first the missionaries tried to protect the rights of the native peoples and urged respect for their culture, greatly to the anger of the conquistadors, though later many succumbed to the greed and corruption which flowed from the riches of a defeated subcontinent. By one means or another the lands were evangelised.

Heading the mission were the Jesuits. Approved by the Pope in 1540 for 'the propagation of the faith', they determined 'in whatsoever the reigning pontiff shall command them, to go forth into lands, among Turks, heathens or heretics . . . without question, condition or reward'. They often began with education, and their schools became centres for the teaching and preaching of scripture, the deepening of spiritual life and the leading of 'missions' – evangelistic ministries, often in remote places, over periods of weeks.

The energy of the Jesuits led them to begin work overseas only months after their foundation. In 1541 Francis Xavier sailed for India. Landing in Goa he travelled to Travancore, Sri Lanka, the Moluccas – and in 1549 to Japan where he learnt the language. Wherever he went he founded churches. Ten years after landing at Goa he died on his way to evangelise China. Though his methods can be criticised with the hindsight of four centuries, it was one of the most extraordinary missionary achievements in history.[12]

The subsequent history of the Church in Japan showed that these were no easy mass conversions. The Church had grown steadily after Xavier's death but in 1587 the government proscribed Christianity and attempted to stamp it out. In 1597, 26 recent converts were crucified, but they were merely the best known of many thousands who were martyred. From 1640 all foreigners were banished from the country and for two centuries the Japanese Church suffered persecution without help from outside. It was not until 1859 that foreigners were allowed to enter the country again; they found thousands of Christians still practising their faith.[13]

But St Francis Xavier was only the best-known missionary. There were others, mainly Jesuits, who evangelised India, China, the islands of Indonesia and penetrated deep into South-East Asia and Northern Africa. They preached and taught with such a deep longing to identify with those they preached to that they adopted local dress and customs wholeheartedly and this became a matter of deep controversy. 'Accommodation' – the adapting of Christian faith and practice to make it more straightforward for those of another culture to become Christians – was practised by many Counter Reformation missionaries including Xavier, de Nobili and Matteo Ricci.[14] It was eventually condemned by eighteenth-century popes[15] but the issue is always present for any evangelist with a longing for people to find Christ.

The Protestant Reformation did not lead to such an explosion of expansion. David Bosch, after a careful examination of the evidence, can only say, '. . . very little happened by way of missionary outreach during the first two centuries after the Reformation'.[16] Catholic contemporaries berated the Protestants for their lack of apostolic zeal: as Cardinal Ballarmine said, 'heretics are never said to have converted either pagans or Jews to the faith, but only to have perverted Christians'.

There were excuses. The Protestants were much taken up with establishing Protestantism in Europe and also with internal wrangling. The Second Coming was expected shortly – Luther had set the date as 1558. But the most significant ecclesiological disincentive to mission was the link with the State. Since Constantine, the State and the Church had been intertwined and the Reformation did not untie that knot. Indeed it seems to have been made into an unalterable law which strangled mission for centuries. Northern Europe did not at this time have colonies like Portugal and Spain, and therefore did not have to face the challenge of whether it was right to take the gospel to those in their domains. It was assumed that mission only applied in a Christian country, i.e. one with a Christian ruler. Without colonies the question of what to do about non-Christians did not arise. When the Protestant nations began to found colonies in the sixteenth century they were faced with the missionary question. The early Puritans saw their responsibility in this: the New England Company was founded in 1649 for work among the native people who had become part of the early British colonies in North America.

Moreover, the Protestants had also quashed that part of the Church from which many evangelistic initiatives sprang. Abolishing the monastic orders cut off the apostolic arm of the Church. It was two centuries until the Protestant Churches were able to produce anything similar to the religious orders in the shape of the voluntary societies. Only they were able to have the single-minded drive and freedom from ecclesiastical interference that missionary work demands.

The significance of this is shown by a small splinter group of the Reformation. The Anabaptists went through a much more thoroughgoing reformation than did the Lutherans, Calvinists and Anglicans. They jettisoned any idea of parochial boundaries and 'wandered for the gospel'.[17] They also stated that there should be a complete break between Church and State. This infuriated the more conservative reformed churches who called them *Schwarmerei* – fanatics. In the light of the fact that the Anabaptists regarded both Catholics and mainline Protestants as pagans, this may be understandable, but in their condemnation they lost sight of the essential emphasis that missionaries should be free from parochial boundaries and dependency on the state.

The fundamental theology of the Reformers spoke much of the apostolic ministry of the Church: indeed it was Voetius (1589–1676) who introduced the idea of the Missio Dei, which is so much in tune with Calvinist thinking. However the cutting edge of evangelism was muted. This is seen in the Reformed handling of the Great Commission of Matthew 28. Most of the Reformers regarded the Commission as having been fulfilled by the apostles and therefore as no longer binding on the Church. When the Dutch theologian Adrian Savaria disagreed and said that Christians could only obtain the promise of 'I am with you always' if they obeyed the command of the preceding verse that they should 'go . . . and make disciples of all nations', he was condemned by both Calvinists and Lutherans.

Many excuses for this lack of missionary work were adduced by the Lutherans and Calvinists of the sixteenth, seventeenth and eighteenth centuries. It was claimed that those overseas were savages and not really human; that they were under God's curse; that the task was too hard; there was too much to do at home; and that it was presumptuous to think the Great Commission applied nowadays. Anyway, God had already made himself known to all nations and so there was no need to do anything: besides, his grace did not work so powerfully as it did in New Testament times.

The Great Commission was not so cursorily dismissed by all Protestants. It was held to remain in full force by the Ana-baptists and by two groups who heralded much. The first was an idea of Justinian van Welz who dreamed that the order of hermit should be revived in a 'Jesus-loving Society': he thought they should wander as the Spirit led them and convert by the impact of their holiness. He was laughed to scorn by the Lutheran Church but, true to his conviction, sailed to Surinam where he died in 1666, leaving no church behind him.

His sad story was not copied by the Moravians. Though severely persecuted, a small group of Hussites had remained in Bohemia since the fifteenth century and after many wanderings settled in Herrnhut near Dresden in 1722 at the invitation of Count Zinzendorf. In 1727 there was a charismatic outbreak in the community with speaking in tongues,[18] prophecy and healings taking place, which in its turn led to a continuous watch of prayer for a hundred years. The community was seen as the *ecclesiola in ecclesiae* – the little community within the Church. Zinzendorf had always had a missionary interest. At the age of 15 he had set up a 'Compact for the Conversion of Pagans' and in 1730, while on a visit to Copenhagen, he met a slave from the West Indies and two Eskimos from Greenland who all begged him to send missionaries. Returning to Herrnhut he put the challenge before the community, who accepted it with enthusiasm.

During the next twenty years missionaries streamed out from this tiny community – to the slaves in the Virgin Islands, to Greenland, Surinam, South Africa, the North American native people, Jamaica and Antigua. Many died but others took their place. Zinzendorf had a horror of churches and their apparatus of organisation and decreed that no churches should be founded by the Moravians but that new converts should be gathered into 'pilgrim houses' under the direct guidance of the Holy Spirit. Like many another reformer who has had the same aversion and the same desire, he found that in fact the 'pilgrim houses' soon became churches, though the word 'church' was resisted for many years.

It has been claimed that the Moravians did more missionary work in these twenty years than had been done by all the Protestant Churches of Europe in the two previous centuries. Certainly their example spurred many others into action (not least John Wesley) and helped to energise the missionary endeavours of the last two centuries.

Communication (Stage 6)

For over three hundred years the Protestant Churches and the Roman Catholics grew apart. A long *history* grew up of bitter dispute and conflict, which included the Massacre of the Huguenots, the penal laws in England, the Thirty Years War, the Gunpowder Plot, and the 'Popish Plot' of Titus Oates. These themselves became matters of controversy and of growing mythology: even today few Protestants fully understand what their forefathers inflicted on Catholics or vice versa, while all too often their own version of the history of these times is kept well polished.

Moreover matters of *doctrine* moved apart. The papal claims became more extreme until they peaked with the ultramontane victories of Vatican I. *Ex cathedra* definitions of faith were few, but those like the declarations on the Assumption and the Immaculate Conception put further barriers between Catholics and Protestants.

Further difficulties came with a divergence of *practice*. Differing understandings of the ministry of women, contraception, and the like, meant that the lifestyles and prejudices of the two Churches became more distinct. Time is no healer in these circumstances: every year that passes exacerbates the situation.

The ecumenical movement began outside Europe. The divisions which had started in Europe had been all too readily exported so that Catholics and Protestants sent missionaries to be in competition with each other. However once abroad, frequently in hostile surroundings, these same missionaries often found that the faith they shared was greater than what divided them. It was put brutally by one woman Protestant missionary at the time of the Congo uprising: 'when you are being raped on the same bed as a Catholic nun and both calling on the same Jesus you find that differences fade'.

From overseas the ecumenical movement spread to Europe. The Edinburgh Missionary Conference of 1910 led, via the International Missionary Council, Life and Work and then Faith and Order, to the eventual setting up of the World Council of Churches in 1948. Communication began, at first slowly and tentatively, with individuals and groups approaching each other hesitantly, often without official backing. Talking started to replace polemic. This greater understanding of each other began to lower the barricades. It was also noticeable that times of spiritual renewal had profound ecumenical implications as Catholics and Protestants prayed together in Jesus Caritas, Cursillo, Focalare and, above all, in the charismatic movement. From this arose a sense of togetherness and understanding which made those involved impatient of church structures and the slow pace of the ecumenical dance.

However, the legacy of three centuries of history, and diverging doctrine and practice, have left formidable obstacles to real convergence. It is often through increasing communication that convergence is achieved. Will it again be pressure from outside Europe that forces Rome, Canterbury and Geneva together at the beginning of the new millennium in the same way as happened about a hundred years ago?

Consequences (Stage 7)

In so sprawling a renewal as the Reformation spread over so many hundreds of years, it is not surprising that there is no single result to be seen.

It is easy enough to see fragmentation (Stage 7a). Group divided into groups, denomination into denominations, apparently endlessly. While this proliferation is mainly on the Protestant side it is also true to a lesser extent of the Catholic

Church as groups have split from the main body to become churches in their own right. Some fragment into tiny ineffective groups, while others grow to a considerable size. Their number is incalculable: no one can be sure how many different groupings there are in the United States, let alone the whole world. One can only be certain that the number this year will be more than last year.

Many churches of the Reformation became denominations (Stage 7b), while some of them, like the Baptists, the Pentecostals, the Anglicans, the Lutherans and the Methodists expanded into worldwide communions.

Assimilation (Stage 7c) has been less obvious in one sense. While there have been examples of Reformation groups being absorbed into the Roman Catholic Church, they have not been numerous or large. What has been remarkable has been the interplay between the Catholics and Protestants as the ecumenical movement has progressed. Many Protestants have become more Catholic in their approach to prayer and liturgy. There has also been a move towards a more 'Catholic' approach to authority: it has become clear that a group of people is needed to 'run' a church, and that there is a pressure for one of that number to act as a spokesperson. This in turn leads to the requirement for a church to have someone from outside to act as an advisor and, if necessary, as a disciplinarian. The naturalness by which bishops, priests and deacons evolve (whatever they may be called) has become obvious to many, though usually without those concerned taking a fully 'catholic' view of those ministries.[19]

Even more significant has been the way in which the Roman Catholic Church has been affected by other churches. One of the insoluble questions of Church history is: 'Would Vatican II have taken place and had the effect it did, had it not been for the contact the Pope and the bishops had had with other Christians?' Vatican II has led, in the eyes of some conservative Roman Catholics, to the 'Protestantisation of the Catholic Church', with its greater recognition of the role of the laity, greater freedom in a vernacular liturgy and use of the Bible, and encouragement of ecumenism. It will be a long time before we can see what the outcome of this will be: we can be sure that there will be no easy solutions.

CONCLUSIONS

Time and tide wait for no one

Renewals which do not begin quickly to communicate with the mainstream find that it becomes more and more difficult with the passing years. We have seen this in the way that the Reformation Churches grew apart from the Roman Catholic Church over the centuries. The example of the relationship between the English Methodist Church and the Church of England is even more depressing: despite the very considerable overlap of practice, theology and understanding between the Churches and their shared life on an island, over time each church has evolved somewhat different ways of doing things and varying patterns of church government.

The passage of time creates wariness. After a divorce or any quarrel the elapse of time causes people to establish a new pattern of life and become set in their emotional reactions. In a local church this means that the congregation polarises into factional camps, and until they can meet at the level of friendship and trust there will always be suspicion. In ecumenical terms there is the fear that one church is trying to 'absorb' the other – particularly if they are of different size.

If there is to be a rapprochement between groups, leaders need to realise that nothing is gained by burying the issues and hoping they will resolve themselves. In this case time does not heal but exacerbates the problems. Local churches need to grasp nettles: the ecumenical movement needs to be more urgent than the stately gavotte which is the current pace.

Renewal and evangelism do not necessarily go hand in hand

We looked particularly at the pace of mission in relation to renewal and found that at the Reformation it was not Strand A which evangelised, but Strand B. We looked at some reasons for this and found that the main one was the ecclesiological link which had been made in Protestantism between a geographical area, political power and mission. The idea of the 'Christian prince' was so strong that the idea of taking the gospel to areas which were not under the control of one of these paragons was beyond comprehension. Nor did this merely concern the nation states which were becoming more self-consciously differentiated in the sixteenth century – it also applied to parochial boundaries, as can be seen in the vituperation hurled at the Anabaptists for overstepping them. Boundaries can be useful and even necessary for pastoral work: but they can be hindrances to evangelism. Whether it is the medieval friars or John Wesley's claim that 'the world is my parish', evangelists inevitably find that they have at times to ignore boundaries – and the church which fails to make this possible will be the poorer.[20]

It is ironic that the Reformation which so emphasised the role of the individual before his or her God should in the field of mission have been so blinkered by a strong sense of the individual-in-community that it could not look outside that community to the needs of others. Only the despised *Schwarmerei* who gave 'enthusiasm' such a bad name were not cramped by their ecclesiology.

Mission needs a stimulus

The breaking away of so much of ecclesiastical Europe meant that the Catholic Church was forced to think outwards – partly in terms of re-evangelising the areas of Europe which had been lost to the 'heretics', and partly in reaching out beyond Europe. However, this was not merely a matter of reconquest: there was a theological imperative, provided especially by the Jesuits, which made missionary work important. The apostolic nature of the Church had always been an important element: many of the early friars had tried to evangelise beyond Christendom, following the famous encounter between St Francis and Sultan al-Kamil in Egypt. The need for mission was made more urgent in the sixteenth century by five elements, two from within the Church and three from outside.

First and foremost, the Counter Reformation made many aware of the preciousness of the gospel. Their deep spirituality led to a longing to share it with all; the reality of their faith shines from the pages of all their writings.

Secondly, the Counter Reformation was all too aware that Catholic Christendom would not necessarily last for ever and had to be reformed and expanded. The capture of Constantinople by the Turks in 1453 had shown that, just as the last of the Moorish kingdoms were being quenched in Spain after a three-century-long struggle, there was a real possibility of being overwhelmed from the east. With the loss of the north of Europe to the Protestants, Catholics realised they might be corralled in a small area of south-west Europe. Undoubtedly there was a degree of paranoia as it seemed to the Catholics that they were in a shrinking enclave: as often happens when boundaries rise between a church and its context, there was an increase of energy.

But things were also happening in the wider world which made mission a possibility. First, the Catholic countries of Spain and Portugal now had a number of colonies with many millions of subject people. Were they to be left to their own practices? The conquistadors, who did not shock easily, were genuinely appalled by the bloody human sacrifices of some of the South American religions.[21] What was to be done about these people spiritually? The answer was to send missionaries. And if the people in the colonies needed Christ, why not those beyond the colonial borders?

Secondly, the real size of the world was beginning to be appreciated. Hitherto the world had hardly been conceived of as much larger than the Romans had thought more than a thousand years before. Now it was seen to be full of possibilities. Maps were still produced with the unknown areas filled with strange mythical creatures, but many people now knew that in reality these lands were inhabited by human beings.

Thirdly, it has to be said that the thrill of adventure drew many to voyage into strange and uncharted countries. The age was one of exploration and novelty, and for many missionaries this was the spiritual counterpoint to political conquest, just as the Victorian missionary expansion had some of the same quality.[22]

Committed individuals need to take the lead

The importance of the Pope in directing missionary effort was considerable. It was his responsibility to attend to the spiritual needs of every human being, and his unique position meant that he had as good a view of the world as anyone. Just as earlier popes in the Dark Ages had directed monks to evangelise England, Germany and Scandinavia, and their twelfth-century successors had protected the preaching friars, so the sixteenth-century popes wished to encourage mission. This was achieved primarily through the Jesuits, who were rightly regarded, and often resented, as being the Pope's favourites and who were sent by him to reconvert the Protestants and evangelise the world. Whatever the personal morals or capabilities of the current pontiff, the fact that he was in a position to direct as well as persuade showed itself in increased missionary activity. This suggests that today, in denominations or in local churches, there needs to be someone (or a small group of motivated people) who has the responsibility for mission and also the power to make something happen.

The importance of there being a small band of committed people who led where others could follow was well illustrated by the Jesuits. It was something which the Protestants were to lack for many years until the Anabaptists and the Moravians taught others what could be done by a few dedicated people in the service of the many. The 'voluntary principle', which came to be so important in mission work, both in Europe and elsewhere, was not learnt until much later. It was not enough to wait for the leadership of churches to do something, especially where no one had primary responsibility for mission: there was a place for the Christian commando unit. We shall see in the next chapter the difficulties which this may cause, but the courage and faith of the early pioneers in mission deserve our admiration.

6 *Renewal Goes West*

There are generally held to have been two American 'Awakenings'. The First or Great Awakening was associated with a general evangelical upsurge in the 1730s–1760s which touched England, Scotland and Germany as well as America. Indeed it was the English clergyman George Whitefield who played a significant part in the American Awakening. It began among the Presbyterians in Pennsylvania and New Jersey and then jumped to Congregationalist and Baptist churches. It is particularly associated with the preaching of Jonathan Edwards,[1] but many others were involved, not least those trained to promote revival[2] in 'the Log College', which later became Princeton University. The Awakening quickly spread amongst the northern states and in the 1740s moved south to Virginia and North Carolina. By the 1750s it was running out of steam and the period of the American Revolution and the founding of the new nation was a time of very low religious vitality. Church membership in 1776 is variously estimated but was not more than 17% of the population and the percentage going to church was much lower – perhaps only 5%.[3] Indeed some have used this figure to claim that the effect of the Great Awakening has been greatly exaggerated and it was really just a number of local revivals which had only a short-term effect.[4] The prevailing theological tone by that time had become liberal, and even unitarian, particularly in Presbyterian and Congregationalist academic circles.

The Second Awakening was more diffuse. It is difficult to be precise but it is generally held to have lasted from the 1790s to the 1820s. It had two particular foci. The first was the camp meeting. At this time the great western plains were being opened up to settlement. The pioneers were spilling out from the eastern seaboard in search of land and riches. But for many of the settlers it was a lonely life, with individual families living in homesteads many miles from any neighbour. Occasionally, when work was slack, often after the harvest was in, people would congregate for buying and selling – and for religion. Since many had come long distances these gatherings could last for two or three weeks, and there would be two or three sermons each day. They generated much fervour – and often a display of wild behaviour which scandalised the upright and the theologically precise. Thus Jedidiah Morse, in 1792, describes the Methodist preachers he had encountered with considerable disdain:

> their mode of preaching is extremely extemporaneous, very loud and animated . . . they appear studiously to avoid connection in their discourses, and are fond of introducing pathetic [ie. sentimental] stories. Their preaching is frequently attended with surprising effect upon their congregation.

Another innovation which caused criticism was the place of women in the revivals. In the pioneering days many women in the west toiled alongside their menfolk, and when it came to religion they were not to be left behind. It was they who did much of the arranging of the camp meetings, they gave hospitality to the circuit riders and cooked endlessly. But it went beyond that: in the west they had a freedom to express their views in ways which would never have been given them in the more respectable east.

The other main element in the Second Awakening was the deliberate engendering of 'revival'. This was not a matter to be left wholly to the Holy Spirit: it was something which could be organised. This is particularly linked with the name of Charles Grandison Finney (1792–1875) who declared, 'religion is the work of man, it is something for man to do'. Missions were arranged in town after town, often in the open air or a vast tent hired for the occasion, and people poured in, at least in part for the entertainment value. There is no doubt that the Second Awakening had an effect. Church membership doubled in the period from 1776–1850.[5]

MILLENNIALISM

Before we look further at how far our hypothesis fits the American scene it is useful to pause and consider an element which had a major influence on the way the American renewal unfolded and on the content of the message which was central to it. In Revelation 20 it is written:

> I saw the souls of those who had been beheaded for their testimony to Jesus and for the word of God ... They came to life and reigned with Christ a thousand years (the rest of the dead did not come to life until the thousand years were ended.) This is the first resurrection ... When the thousand years are ended, Satan will be released from prison and will come out to deceive the nations ...[6]

Millennialism is difficult to define but enormous in motivational power. It can probably be best seen as 'a longing for a new and better world where God is supreme'. In the Early Church the question as to whether or not Christ would literally return for a thousand-year reign in fulfilment of Revelation 20 was much debated. The idea of a messianic kingdom had a Jewish origin: 4 Ezra 7:28 says that it would last for 400 years.[7] The return of Christ for a thousand-year reign was believed in by Irenaeus of Lyons (c.130–c.200) and by Tertullian (c.160–c.225). However, it was rejected by Eastern theologians. Thus the Greek writer Hippolytus (c.170–c.236) saw it as a poetic illustration of the grandeur of the heavenly kingdom rather than a literal earthly millennium.

It has to be said that the 'amillennialism' propounded by Hippolytus has had surprisingly few adherents, except among scholars and those of a liberal point of view. This may suggest that millennialism speaks to some depth of the human heart

which longs for a better future where good will triumph and
evil be shown up for what it is. It is not surprising that some
of its roots are in the Jewish thinking of the last centuries BC
when the Jews were enduring much from conquest and cruelty.
The psalmist's cry,

> Why, O Lord, do you stand far off?
> Why do you hide yourself in times of trouble?[8]

is one echoed by anyone of faith, and the thought of a golden
age to come is comforting – 'there really will come a time when
the righteous are at peace and the evil get what is coming to
them'.

But the idea of a millennium is not enough. There was, and is,
a debate of deep fervour for some, as to when the millennium will
arrive and what will happen when it does. In Reformation theology although there was a reaction against excessive futurology
there was also a sense that something was about to happen. Calvin
thought the world was well into the 'third (and final) age' of
the Church.[9] In eighteenth-century evangelical theology there also
arose the belief that the millennium would come only when certain preconditions had been met – the coming of the 'fullness
of the Gentiles' into the Church (often accompanied by a belief
in the conversion of the Jews). Thus millennarianism came to be
allied to mission. Indeed many early evangelists were motivated by the idea that they were taking part in this great plan
of God: 'shall we remain idle in this harvest time of the world?'[10]
One of the preaching tags of those days was 'Bring back the King'.

Pre-millennialists believe that when Christ returns all those in
Christ, both dead and alive at the time, will reign with Christ
for a millennium, after which Satan will be released for a short
time. *Post-millennialists* believe that Christ will return after a
thousand years. What happens during the thousand years is
debated: for some it is the triumph of the gospel throughout
the world, for others a time of unparalleled peace.

The distinctions between the two outlooks are profound. The
chart opposite sets out, somewhat crudely, the beliefs in their
developed modern form.

Pre-millennialism

- Pessimistic about the world and the fate of non-Christians.
- Teaches separation from the world.

- Justification by grace through faith lays more emphasis on God's work of grace than on human faith.
- A subjective view is taken of experience with emphasis on holiness and closeness to God.

Post-millennialism

- Optimistic about the world.

- The Church's task is to bring in the Kingdom. There should be a close link between Church and State (both Lutheran Erastianism and Calvinist thinking about theocracy). Missionary work is of the greatest importance.
- Justification lays much stress upon the human need to respond to God.

- The world needs us to work and achieve.

As the years passed in the nineteenth century three other distinctions evolved:

- The individual before God is all-important: religion is primarily a private matter of opinion rather than a matter of fact.
- There is an emphasis on the private interpretation of Scripture.

- Politically and ethically conservative.

- The social context is the way to work for God: the 'Social Gospel' preached a benign God.[11]

- The world as well as Scripture sets the agenda. A more liberal view of Scripture is taken.
- Politically and ethically liberal with a strong belief in democracy.

In the United States there was not much disagreement between pre- and post-millennialists before the end of the Second Awakening: indeed the terms 'pre-millennial' and 'post-millennial' were not used until the 1840s. It was then that the desire of small groups of Christians for precise definitions led to what has been called 'the era of controversy'. The theological divisions were exacerbated by current political implications: the early pre-millennialists preached withdrawal from the world and from campaigning about such issues as slavery; the post-millennialists insisted that the Church could not let the world go to hell without trying to prevent it. However, political withdrawal by the pre-millennialists has not proved sustainable in an activist society and they have become the most vociferous of all in their condemnation of Communism and anything which threatens the American way of life, and most wary of anything which could be considered to be of social concern.[12]

Generally speaking, the Christian leaders of the Awakenings were post-millennialists. People like Jonathan Edwards emphasised the need to build the Kingdom, and many of them took a stoutly progressive line on slavery and the treatment of the poor.[13] Most of them were children of Calvin: they were also, often without realising it, children of the Enlightenment and of America. The Enlightenment gave them their focus upon the human being as an autonomous individual with 'certain unalienable Rights ... Life, Liberty and the Pursuit of Happiness', which is the progressive view of the Declaration of Independence: it is hardly classic Calvinism. America presented them with a place of endless possibilities, optimism and activity which did not chime easily with the gloomier parts of Calvin's teaching. They were not prepared to accept the weak excuses of the Reformers about mission – they were to be evangelists to the world. The innate activism and optimism of early-nineteenth-century America made post-millennialism congenial. Thus the post-millennialists' Calvinism was much modified, and, in practice, their offer of salvation to any who would repent and believe went far beyond Calvin into Arminianism.[14]

However, the disconcerting and disappointing period of

reconstruction after the Civil War showed that not all things could be done by human effort and a conservative reaction towards the end of the nineteenth century once again brought pre-millennialism to the fore.[15] This in turn led to the fundamentalist controversy and the association of so much of American evangelicalism with right-wing politics.[16]

THE HYPOTHESIS

Stage 1: Renewal

We do not need to discuss in detail the nature of the initial renewal. It was obvious enough to contemporaries, and was often seen as occurring spontaneously under the direction of the Holy Spirit, especially in its early days.

Stage 2: Conflict

The ensuing conflict came from two directions – from outside the revival movements and also from within.

The first was an attack upon the revivals by the more staid members of the theological establishment. As we have seen, they criticised the preaching, but it was not only that. They disliked the whole idea of itinerancy – preachers wandering wherever they wished. This was particularly directed at George Whitefield. He had come from England in 1736, returned home in order to receive priest's orders in the Church of England, and then came back as a preacher in 1739. He spoke to great crowds throughout New England without much concern for local churches or leaders. The conservatives demanded that the local pastor should have the right to bar any preacher if he wanted to. They were not heeded: besides the impossibility of such a requirement in a rapidly growing new country, the whole spirit of the young American democracy was against them.

The other criticism from outside concentrated on the strange goings-on at the meetings. In the First Awakening there had been allegations of disorder and of the exercise of what we would now describe as charismatic gifts. Jonathan Edwards had to write a paper 'The Distinguishing Marks of a Work of the Spirit of God' in 1741 to answer the critics. In it he admitted that there were things which were unbecoming but put a strong scriptural mark alongside those which he felt were the work of the Holy Spirit. In the Second Awakening strange happenings were much more common, particularly at the camp meetings. The west was still wild at the end of the eighteenth century, and the gatherings matched the culture. Particularly famous (or notorious) were the Cane Ridge meetings of 1800, from which we have the record of two observers.

Peter Cartwright was a Methodist circuit rider[17] and so part of the scene he describes. In one passage he refers to what would today be described as 'resting in the Spirit': 'I have seen more than a hundred sinners fall like dead men under one powerful sermon'. Other witnesses testify to the same phenomenon, which also occurred at many of John Wesley's meetings.

That this preaching had a more than emotional appeal comes from Cartwright's description of the conversion of 'Sister S.':

> She then and there covenanted with the Lord, if he would give her the blessing, she would give up her slaves and set them free. She said this covenant had hardly been made one moment, when God filled her soul with such an overwhelming sense of Divine love, that she did not really know whether she was in or out of the body.

Barton Stone is a more objective, though not unsympathetic, observer. Here he describes the 'jerks':

> I have seen the person stand in one place and jerk backward and forward in quick succession . . . I have enquired of those so affected. They could not account for it; but some have told me that those were among the happiest seasons of their lives.

He goes on to describe 'the dancing exercise', 'the barking exercise', 'the laughing exercise' and 'the singing exercise'.

It may not be surprising that, as Cartwright says, 'some

sinners mocked, some of the old dry professors opposed, some of the old starched Presbyterian preachers preached against these exercises, but still the work went on . . .'. Many were scandalised, and by the time that tales of these happenings reached the east coast seminaries they had been considerably embellished. In these colleges the cool deism of the eighteenth century was the predominant theological flavour – as is well represented by the references to 'Nature's God' and the 'Creator' in the Declaration of Independence. The Congregationalists had for some time had a number of churches and seminaries which had adopted an Arian Christology, and were in effect, Unitarian. The appointment of the liberal Henry Ware as Professor of Divinity at Harvard in 1805 caused further widespread conservative concern since it showed that many other colleges, though officially sponsored by mainstream denominations, were becoming unitarian in their teaching.

Inevitably the full-blooded nature of revivalist religion caused horror and disdain among the academic establishment. The Harvard faculty were so alarmed that in 1844 they produced a 'Testimony against the Revd. George Whitefield and his conduct'. They criticised his lack of academic ability to teach – 'he hath not any superior Talent at Instructing the mind, or showing the Force and Energy of those Arguments for a Religious Life which are directed to in the everlasting Gospel'. It is doubtful if Whitefield was perturbed: he felt himself called to preach the gospel not to argue about it. Further, he was reaching the ordinary working people of America in a way which the college professors were manifestly failing to do. He used homespun preaching to the illiterate, to the immigrants who did not have English as their first language, and to those who understood emotions and stories but not concepts. 'The churching of America was accomplished by aggressive churches committed to a vivid otherworldliness.'[18]

Another area of conflict arose within the Awakening movement itself. The question occurred during the First Awakening but became more insistent during the Second: how far should the revivals be organised? Some, especially those from the

Pietist tradition from Europe, wished to wait upon the Spirit in prayer and leave the timing and the pattern of God's working in people's lives up to him. Certainly the earliest episodes of the Awakenings seem to have been spontaneous outpourings of the Holy Spirit, but American organisational ability soon began to systematise and then to organise.

The process of conversion was soon dissected and turned into a blueprint. Charles Finney rightly said that all were equally sinners before God, but the dangerous implication was drawn that therefore everyone could be treated in the same way. Thus the potential convert was expected to follow certain clearly marked-out steps. The process began with a state of 'concern' about the state of oneself before God. This led to the need for 'inquiry' into the truths of the gospel. A knowledge of these led to 'anxiety' about the possibility of eternal damnation, which in turn led to 'conviction' – the knowledge that nothing one could do would earn salvation except the surrender of oneself to God. This climaxed in the moment of conversion when the repentant sinner (often in tears) 'received Christ' at the 'anxious bench' at the front of the meeting. This conversion had to be sudden and datable so that the believer could look back and know that on such and such a day he or she had found God. There was such emphasis on the will of the person concerned that faith tended to become something human beings could do rather than being a gift of God: as Finney said 'sinners are bound to change their own heart'. If we respond to God in a certain way, God is constrained by his own promises (in the Bible) to acknowledge this by granting forgiveness. In practice, Calvinist predestination was discarded for a doctrine close to fideism – that faith is no more than the human decision to trust God.

Here there was a pattern which could be universally applied and which became the stock in trade of the 'plain-speaking' revivalist preacher, for preaching came to be seen as almost the only way in which people could hear the gospel and be invited to respond. The preaching itself became stereotyped: in it can be seen Charles Finney's early skills as a lawyer, for his words often have the flavour of an address to a jury by someone pleading for and awaiting their verdict.

Another feature was that the revivals were themselves organised. The camp meetings had to be well programmed as thousands of people came together at a remote spot. It was all very homespun but the logistics were formidable and the preachers had to be up to the expectation's heaped upon them. Charles Finney in particular left nothing to chance: he gave detailed 'new measures' about where to hold a revival, what arrangements had to be made for the meeting place, the training of the counsellors, the hymns that were to be sung (not too many), the notices (not extensive) and the feeding which would be required. After a while the leaders of the revivals realised the central importance of preaching and set up colleges to give a training to prospective preachers which went far beyond that of the Log College of the First Awakening. The prospective preachers were educated in the content and the practice of preaching, for these were to be the leaders of new revivals. Finney's writings, such as his immensely influential 'Lectures on Revivals' (1835) were designed for the men who would copy his methods.

The American 'Crusade' had been born. It joined together the expected experience of conversion with the well-organised meeting. This led to 'mass' evangelism. There is a direct line from Finney, who has been called 'the first of the professional evangelists', through Moody, Billy Sunday and many others to the Billy Graham Organisation of today. Carefully crafted meetings encourage a carefully crafted response from those who come. With all its deficiencies, it has yet been of value to many tens of thousands of people. The danger, both then and now, is that it can be seen as the chief form, or even the only form, of evangelism. Into its pattern all have to be shoehorned. It has to be said that it does not cater for those who come to God by another pathway.

Revivalism is often seen as an entirely Protestant phenomenon. However, several Roman Catholic orders copied the pattern of the Protestant 'revivals'. The Redemptorists led nearly 4000 missions in the period from 1860–1890, and their most famous preacher, Fr. Weninger, once preached 1000 sermons in a year. A continuing relic of this in many Catholic American parishes is the 'confraternity', which in a Protestant church would be called more straightforwardly 'a prayer meeting'.

Stage 3: Networking

The strong individualism and the vast distances of America made networking difficult. However, networking is encouraged if there is a common perceived enemy, and for many of the revivalists this enemy was the 'liberal' theologians. Often they were perceived as being a product of the eastern seaboard and the westerners had the traditional scorn of hardbitten pioneers for the soft-living and well-educated town dwellers.

But another factor was at work. The Reformation principle concerning the supreme significance of the autonomous human being before God, coupled with the powerful individualism of the United States, meant that each person sought to steer their own destiny. Further, they did this without waiting for permission from anyone, certainly not from the leaders of the existing denominations who were generally perceived as being liberal. Additionally the prevalent post-millennialist optimism stirred people into action: if they saw that something needed doing, they did it themselves. This voluntaryism meant that there was a proliferation of societies, associations, fellowships and the like. They catered for multitudinous purposes – temperance, the abolition of slavery, prison reform, education, hospitals, 'the reform of manners'. Nearly all of them had a religious basis, and many of them had revivalist roots. At the time of the Reformation it was thought that only the official Church, whether Protestant or Catholic, could initiate anything: America showed that far, far more could be done by a small group of people dedicated to a cause.

Some of these groupings became denominations, but many tried to create a new phenomenon: the non-denominational

church. Count Zinzendorf had tried to cut the Church out of
the gospel but had not succeeded. The experiment was tried
again in America many times over. It seldom worked: the
church in some form or other kept reappearing. Time and again
these grouping either became churches themselves with the full
panoply of denominational budgets, headquarters and buildings, or they became para-church organisations which worked
alongside the churches.

'Voluntaryism'[19] is the view that the Church should be organised by action which is free and sacrificial and should not be
dependent upon professionals or hierarchies. It was a development which contributed vast energy to the life of the Church
as a whole but at the cost of an immense number of splinter
groups, sects and new religions. As George Marsden says about
the growth in the number of denominations, 'it is the product of
a combination of European churchly tradition, ethnic loyalties,
pietism, sectarianism and American free enterprise'.[20]

The first two-thirds of the nineteenth century saw all too
many of these sects arising on the edge of the Christian faith or
beyond. Theosophy, spiritualism in its modern form, Christian
Science, Seventh Day Adventism, Mormonism and Jehovah's
Witnesses are just those which remain today: there were many
others which have long since dwindled to nothing. Some had
Christian roots, while others came from the contemporary
interest in Eastern faiths and in spiritism.[21]

Stage 4: Definition

It was fear of liberalism which caused the 'age of controversy'
in the 1820s and beyond. There had been considerable ecumenical co-operation in the years succeeding Independence,
but the Second Awakening brought tensions to the surface. On
the one hand there was the raw, hot-blooded religion of the
revivalists with not a theological nuance in sight; on the other
there were the educated theologians, many of whom were so
submerged in the Enlightenment and the prevailing deism that
they had reduced the Christian faith to a shell without a living

Christ or a life-changing gospel. Social, ethnic and geographical divides meant that any accommodation between the two sides was unlikely, and the writings of the time breathe an impatience with their opponents which was unlikely to lead to compromise. In particular, the Holiness movement was motivated in part by a longing for a purer form of Christian worship and living, in part by a hatred of liberalism, and in part by exasperation at the slow pace of negotiations. It led to many different new denominations, among them the Church of the Nazarene and the Free Methodists.

Compromise was not something that the revivalists were prepared to countenance. Indeed each group started to create their own Statement of Faith. They had to define themselves over against other conservative groups as well as the abhorred liberals. Each one therefore tended to become more precise, more conservative and more antagonistic to those who believed differently from themselves. As Neibuhr (1892–1971) wrote about the religious groups of this period:

> they confused themselves with their cause and began to promote themselves, identifying the Kingdom of Christ with the practices and doctrines prevailing in the group . . . Every religious society became intent upon promoting its own particular type of work . . . the more attention was concentrated upon the church the greater became the tendency toward schism.[22]

The scene was set for the rise of fundamentalism in the late nineteenth century, with its strongly pre-millennialist outlook and siege mentality.

Yet another element in the ferment was the growing number of ethnically based churches. As new immigrants poured in from the countries of the Old World they brought their own church practice, and often their own clergy. Different shades of Orthodox, Lutherans, Roman Catholics and others set up their own churches, many of which used their home languages. They also brought over their European divisions: thus the Danish

Pietist immigrant congregations were known as 'the Sad Danes', and the anti-Pietists as 'the Happy Danes'.

All this made for a rich and bewildering mix. American free enterprise led to open competition between the churches, with each of them seeking to exhibit how they were different from and better than others. It was not, and is not, a very edifying scene – but it is certainly dynamic.

Stage 5: Divergence

In America as a whole, with no established or even predominant church, there was no mainstream orthodoxy from which to diverge, so this element within the hypothesis is more complex. However, the phenomenon of divergence has been illustrated time and again as renewals have occurred within such traditional churches as the Roman Catholic, Lutheran, Episcopalian, Baptist and the like. Indeed the story of the American church is the story of this process, which has been called 'overtaking on the right' because nearly always the new grouping has tended to be more conservative in theology and less wedded to denominational niceties than the mainstream. Some within each denomination have remained within it and fought their corner, while others have engaged in what Richard Lovelace calls 'therapeutic separation'.[23]

Stage 6: Communication

Communication between Strand B and the mainstream Church has meant that frequently the children of renewal movements influence the whole and are ultimately absorbed again. However, the communication in America between Strand A churches and their roots are few indeed. The competitive spirit which is so marked ensures that churches tend to co-operate only infrequently; there may be friendliness at a personal level but it seldom translates into real ecumenism or mission together.[24]

Stage 7: Consequences

In so vast and sprawling a church picture as that found in the United States it is not surprising that every possible outcome of renewal has come to pass not once but many times over. Often groups have fragmented again and again, each becoming smaller and less able to forward the Kingdom of God because of their need to maintain their internal cohesion and because of their numerical weakness. Other groups are assimilated back into their mainstream.

However the most usual consequence has been the formation of new denominations. The US has spawned more denominations than any other country. In a marketplace of ideas which is as brash as America's, every church has to make itself heard. This means that a new church has to market itself with panache if members are to be drawn to it. The result is that as soon as a new group forms it looks to organise, if possible get airtime, and make itself known. For churches which fail – and it has to be remembered that the average-size church in America has only 120 members – the end is to become a furniture store.

Whether this process is good or bad for the Kingdom of God is hard to say. On the one hand the United States is the only developed country with a Christian background which has managed to *increase* its church-going population despite secularisation and urbanisation, in sharp contrast with the churches of Europe and Australasia. On the other hand it has exported its denominations around the world so that the Christian body in many countries is divided and ineffective.

CONCLUSIONS

The effect of eschatology

The reverberations of millennialism are obvious. The expectation that the world is to be radically changed by an irruption of God in the near future was a major element in the American Awakenings. It was a motive for mission and for energy within the church.

But, as we have seen, millennialism comes in two flavours. The more optimistic post-millennialism which was most in favour during the Awakenings became subsumed into the liberal American dream of progress and expansion. The pessimism of pre-millennialism, which has been predominant during the past 150 years, has often led to a ghetto-like quality in much of American religious life, even when it has been outwardly successful in terms of church membership.

It is hard to avoid the conclusion that the various forms of millennialism have largely mirrored the current mood of the country. The period after the War of Independence when all things were possible was a naturally post-millennial age. The slaughter and hatreds of the Civil War and the uneasy time of reconstruction afterwards led to a lack of self-confidence which was reflected in the prevailing pre-millennialism. This pre-millennialism continued during the twentieth century (among evangelicals) as the two world wars, the Wall Street crash and Vietnam continued to foster the largely pessimistic national attitude. However, there has been a move back to a post-millennial position in the past twenty years when the natural buoyancy and political engagement of the American people have reasserted themselves during a period of relative calm and economic growth.

Whatever the reasons for them, the two stances within the Christian Church are clear-cut. One is life-enhancing, seeing the work of God the Creator in all things; the other is life-denying, seeing the world around as intrinsically hostile – through either direct persecution or subversion. The paranoia which is never far from the surface of the latter all too easily descends into conspiracy theories: this can readily be seen in the United States where ideas about the ten-horned beast of Revelation 13 mingle with thoughts of the crypto-Communists in the Federal Government, the evil of the European Community and that satanic world government, the United Nations.[25] These positions are by no means necessarily tied to the various forms of millennialism but they have proved convenient flags around which many evangelical Christians have gathered – often in order to glare at each other.

Renewals have differed in their attitude. Some have been life-accepting, ready to see God in all things; others have wished to withdraw from the evil temptations of the world. As we saw in Chapter 2, it is the followers of the latter who feel most isolated and are therefore most ready to condemn others, to define their position with greatest rigidity, to have a narrow interpretation of Christian belief and behaviour and the highest boundary between themselves and their context. Pre-millenial renewal therefore tends to result in fragmentation and a multiplicity of different groups and denominations. However, it has to be said that the energy-level of such sects will be higher than the more life-affirming groups. If a group of people believe that the world is shortly going to end and that the number of the saved will be few, there is a strong motivation for a whirlwind of activity in seeking to bring as many as possible into the safety of Christ before the deadline. The tension is heightened even more if a definite date has been set on which the world will end – the ticking clock sets an ever nearing terminus. This may not be as dangerous for the future of a renewal as might be expected since, even if the world does not end as predicted, it does not necessarily lead to the movement's collapse. As we have seen in Chapter 2, 'dissonance theory' suggests that such non-events can be coped with as long as the grouping remains a sect: if it has become a church (in sociological terms) many disillusioned members will leave.

The future of such a life-denying group is not difficult to forecast. The passing of time will tend to erode the height of the boundary, the energy level will diminish and the sect transmute into a church. There are very few groups which can keep up the level of constant activity which a sect often requires. Indeed, the evidence from modern sects suggests that the only way this process can be halted is if adherents are kept apart from the world in a closed community where there is constant reinforcement of the teaching that the world is evil and the group is good. Without this reinforcing of the boundary exhaustion intervenes and the sect starts to become a church.

The more relaxed, life-affirming renewals have fewer sticking points of principle, less need for close definitions and a more genial attitude to the world. They have a lower boundary and hence mix more easily with those around. Therefore the energy level will be lower and the degree of activity less frenetic. On the other hand the staying power will be greater, and it will remain when the feverishly active sect has long since disappeared.

Theological dispute

The American Awakenings present us with extremes of liberalism and conservatism. The liberal 'establishment' was often consciously Arian in theology,[26] had a distaste for 'enthusiasm' and was at home with the European writers like Rousseau, Kant and Hume. Their followers came from the eastern states, were well educated and urbane. Revivalist preachers, on the other hand, were unsophisticated in their theology, their behaviour and their attitudes. Any meeting of minds was unlikely.

The result was a fear and detestation of 'liberals' which entered the evangelical (and some Roman Catholic) thinking of the American Church. None of the new sects could be seen to give an inch to the liberals, with the result that denominational constitutions were drawn up which sought to banish any whiff of liberalism – and often went far beyond the Bible. It was also perceived that many liberals were academics and this in turn led to a fear of scholarship and adventurous thinking. Conservatives therefore kept away from colleges – unless these were under their own control, with the result that the phenomenon of sectarian colleges is still a major factor in the American scene.[27]

On the liberal wing of the Church the utter rejection they received did not encourage them to explore what they could learn from the revivalists. There was, and all too often still is, no meeting of minds, which has meant that denominations are often unable to co-operate together. Further, in mainstream denominations like the Methodists, Episcopalians and Roman Catholics, where there is more than one point of view within each church, there is often an unhelpful polarisation within the denomination. Renewals cast long shadows.

Organise or pray

The reason why the American Awakenings are still significant is the fact that they came to be organised in such a way that they could be replicated. As we have seen, this led to modern 'mass' evangelism.

There are three levels of organisation which are possible for a renewal:

1. Every renewal has to have a minimum degree of organis-ation if people are to gather in a certain place at a certain time. Moreover, if news of it is to travel, communications have to be arranged. Occasionally renewals have tried to 'leave it all to the Holy Spirit' but this is no more successful than the missionary endeavours of the Reformation, and for the same reason.[28]
2. The movement can seek to further its cause by organising meetings, sending out literature, praying and working. But it may be content to produce a second generation of the renewal who are not clones of the first: indeed it can rejoice in their variety as an illustration of the myriad ways in which God works in human lives.
3. The renewal can attempt to replicate itself by so circumscri-bing the way in which it is organised that it tries to produce a second generation who think the same, act the same and often dress in the same way as the first, and who are open only to the same winds of the Spirit.

It is the suspicion that some American renewals and types of evangelism have fallen into the last organisational pattern that makes many people uneasy. This is the reason why that ener-getic lawyer, Charles Finney, is still a controversial figure. For some he was trying to manipulate the Holy Spirit; while for others he was ensuring that the greatest number of people heard the gospel: both may be true.

Voluntaryism

The extraordinary outburst of energy in the Church which can stem from the voluntary principle is seen supremely in America. The exuberance of American life, its get-up-and-go and its democratic system lends itself to independent action.[29]

We have seen something of this ardour in the New Testament and its aftermath, in the mendicant orders and in the Anabaptists and the *Schwarmerei*. It is difficult to see how any renewal can begin without at least one person being prepared to step out of line and to gather others around them. This is as true in a local church as it is on a national level.

The dangers of this approach are manifest and are clearly seen in the New Testament: people may be self-deluded as to what God expects of them; they may be led astray by charlatans; pride may spoil what has been started in the Spirit; leaders may quarrel. Jonathan Edwards was very aware of the possibility of pride among what he described as the 'weeds in revivalism':

> Spiritual pride is very apt to suspect others, to find fault with other saints that they are low in grace . . . being quick to discern their deficiencies.

> Spiritual pride takes great notice of opposition and injuries that are received and is apt to be much taking notice of their aggravations either with an air of bitterness or contempt.

> Pride can move awakened believers to censorious attacks on other Christians, a lack of meekness in rebuking those who really need it and a hair-trigger readiness to separate from those less holy or less orthodox.[30]

Yet, when all the faults have been taken into consideration, it is precisely this voluntaryism which, humanly speaking, led to the foundation of the Church in the first place, has sustained it down the centuries and gives it adventure and sparkle today.

Non-denominationalism

Having seen it tried by Count Zinzendorf, by many groupings in the American Awakenings, and more recently by the New Churches, one can only say that it does not work. The longing to separate Christ from 'his leprous Bride' is understandable, not least in evangelism where the desire to offer Christ and Christ alone is powerful. Few Christians do not have a love-hate relationship with the Church, but the Church obstinately refuses to go away. It appears to be a fact of Christian human nature that if any group of people get together they will sooner or later, however hard they try not to, form a church. They may give their group another title but it is still a church. Indeed there is a danger that if they deny that they are a church, the group may come to believe that they, and they alone, form the true Body of Christ.

More important is the New Testament emphasis on the significance of the Church in the purposes of God. Christians would do well to accept the Church for what it is and how it is portrayed in the Bible – at some times foolishly glorious and at others gloriously foolish.

Charismatic happenings

The camp meetings were the stage for the unusual and the downright strange. We have heard the testimony of Peter Cartwright and Barton Stone. Cartwright was sure that some of the happenings were merely copied by those who were at the meetings – 'sympathetic feeling', especially among the 'weak-minded, ignorant and superstitious'. But some actions were 'perfectly involuntary'.

The academics poured scorn, and many ordinary Christians were scandalised (the Episcopalian Church grew at this time as they were joined by the disaffected from revivalist churches).

But many others were helped, others were made aware of the presence of God, and many were guided in their private and public prayer. Certainly those churches (mainly Baptist and Methodist) most closely identified with the Awakenings grew massively in numbers, especially during the Second Awakening.

Charismatic phenomena can be discerned from the New Testament onwards and became central to the Montanist renewal. (Nor are they confined to the Christian religion.) Some have seen them as signs of peculiar holiness, and others as a sign of soft-headedness. They tend to occur when there is freedom and a keen sense of the presence of God. It may be instructive that while there were instances of these phenomena in Finney's revival meetings, it was not encouraged and soon died out.

The New Testament is our wise guide. The reality of the presence of God is manifest in the congregation, and this presence can be seen at times in signs and wonders both by his people and by those outside the Church. On the one hand, says Paul, do not quench the Spirit or forbid speaking in tongues. On the other, there is time and place for everything for God is a God of order.[31]

Paul is also well aware of the dangers of those who pretend they have special powers and lead followers astray. Weber alludes to the claiming of such powers as an element of human charisma (using his terminology), and it is deadly dangerous if it is not derived from Christ and consecrated to him.

7 Renewal in Today's World

The new millennium is a hinge point – not because there is anything magical in the date but because a new paradigm seems to be emerging. New ways of thinking, new ways of behaving, new possibilities spread before us or our children.

Renewal within the Church has to operate within its context, and we have seen time and again how political, economic and ecclesiastical factors have influenced the course of a renewal. The Cluniac renaissance of monasticism was spurred by a resurgent Europe and the growth in the power of the papacy. More significant still are the intellectual and theological attitudes current at the time of the renewal. Calvinist and Lutheran ecclesiology prevented missionary work by the churches of the Reformation for many years. The American Awakenings and their aftermath were shaped by the Enlightenment and its thinking at least as much as by the self-confidence of a new nation.

Any present-day renewal has to operate in a scene where modernism and post-modernism dictate the way we think and act. The duality leaves many people operating in two worlds – the one logical, rational and rather dull, the other often irrational but much more fun. We have already seen the Church operating in a multi-cultural situation when it adapted to both the Jewish and the Gentile worlds: the same challenge faces Western Christianity today. Help may come from overseas, for the churches of Asia, Africa and South America have been in such multi-cultural situations for generations, and have combined the pressures of their traditonal culture with those of Westernisation, often at a time of disturbing political transition.

THE SHAKING OF THE FOUNDATIONS

It is a truism that the time is out of joint. Isaiah speaks of God's sovereignty in his generation:

> The windows of heaven are opened,
> and the foundations of the earth tremble.
> The earth is utterly broken,
> the earth is torn asunder,
> the earth is violently shaken . . .

> Then the moon will be abashed,
> and the sun ashamed:
> for the Lord of Hosts will reign on Mount Zion
>   and in Jerusalem,
> and before his elders he will manifest his glory.[1]

In every age people have tended to see their present as being less secure than their past. In the new millennium we have some right to claim that this instability is a reality. First, the private lives of people are less secure: families split, relationships degenerate into serial marriage or no marriage at all. The workplace is not the secure place it once was when people worked behind a bank counter or down a coal mine until they were pensioned off. Secondly, the very nature of relationships is being questioned. Between men and women there swirl a multitude of uncertainties which introduce self-doubt into many lives. Shopping, travelling and, above all, the interchange of information have changed radically. While writing this book I have been able to consult, via the web, university libraries in Australia, Germany, America and the UK without stirring from my chair.

But that is merely superficial. There is also a profound change in the very civilisation we inhabit. Culture has been defined as 'what happens around here'. It is the air we breathe, often unexamined, and either noxious or life-giving. The picture on the jigsaw is changing even as we are trying to piece it together. A time of paradigm-shift is a time of profound uncertainty. In the past such dislodgement of the boundary posts has taken several generations to come about: today it seems to happen within a single generation. As the Deuteronomic law says:

> Cursed be anyone who moves a neighbour's landmark.
> All the people shall say 'Amen'.[2]

POST-MODERNISM

What is also changing is the way we think. While I can consult a library on the other side of the planet at the press of a computer key, half the population of the world have never used a phone. The contrasts between rich and poor widen, as do the differences between the information-rich and the information-poor. And many blame the 'progress' which modernism has contrived and which does not seem to have a human face.

Till recently we were in thrall to modernism. In this hard-edged, shadowless universe reason was paramount and scientific progress was bringing us to a bright new world which did not need God, who did not exist anyway. Faith was foolish because it was irrational, the Bible was just another old book, the Church a gathering of the deluded. One post-modernist guru says, 'we are now awakening from the nightmare of modernity, with its manipulative reason and fetish of totality'.

It was in architecture that the word post-modernism came into common use[3] for the modernist architecture common in the 1960s was seen most often in the tower blocks and glass-clad office buildings which came to dominate many cities across the world. It was rightly felt that the scale of these vast buildings dwarfed those who lived and worked in them and a new style of architecture, more human in scale, more user-friendly and less grandiose came to be designated as post-modernist. Architects used an amalgam of styles from the past, especially the classical and the baroque, to create an ironic effect which was intended to bring a smile to our lips.

What is post-modernism? The answer hangs on a hyphen. If the word is written 'postmodernism' it suggests that there is a coherent body of thinking, that there are books which are seen as seminal and experts who can impart the new wisdom. But when the word is written correctly, as 'post-modernism', it is no more than descriptive. It critiques modernism but puts nothing definite in its place. It glories in its ambiguity, its fuzziness, its lack of certainty – for it will have nothing to do with a modernism which is clear-cut, mechanical and cold.[4]

Nevertheless, while there is no fixed body of dogma, post-modernism has certain characteristics. We need to see what impact these might have on renewal movements.

Post-modernism is like a jackdaw[5]

Post-modernism picks up everything, examines it cursorily and puts it in its undifferentiated memory bank. It is like a visit to the supermarket: you pick up a tin of this, a packet of that, a carton of something else and put them in your trolley. In the post-modern supermarket there is a large section of the store marked 'Spirituality' with a bewildering range of goods on offer, for unlike modernism, post-modernism accepts and provides for the spiritual side of human nature. But it is an odd assortment and you may collect in your mental trolley an idea from Hindu mythology, a half-forgotten thought from Christianity, an idea read in a magazine, together with a belief in the power of crystals and little green men. The ideas do not need to hang together – indeed post-modernism delights in paradox. Any attempt to construct a pattern which makes a whole picture is suspect for it might form a dreaded 'meta-narrative' – an attempt to explain everything. This is something abhorred by the post-modernist, whether it is a religious explanation of existence like those of Islam or Christianity, or a political one like communism or capitalism, or a philosophical viewpoint like the systems of Kant or Hegel.

Post-modernism values the spiritual side of humanity: as Eugene Ionesco said in the *Theatre of the Absurd*:

When man is cut off from his religious, metaphysical and transcendental roots, he is lost, everything he does becomes senseless, absurd, useless, is nipped in the bud ... the comic alone is capable of giving us the strength to bear the tragedy of existence.

In some ways this is fertile ground for renewals for post-modernism is less suspicious of fresh things. New ideas are eagerly explored: like Luke's wry comment on the Athenians, postmodernists who would 'spend all their time in nothing but telling or hearing something new'.[6] But the shelf life of novelty is depressingly short. Yesterday's idea is dead. Nevertheless it means that a new concept is able to get an airing and be discussed: it may even be able to make its way and become established. The same tendency can be seen in the life of the Church: new ideas fountain forth, the great majority of which are discarded but a few are widely adopted and are able to make an impact. Bandwagons roll over the horizon, most of which are almost forgotten a few years later, but some take root and are fruitful. Among recent examples in the charismatic movement there have been power evangelism, Toronto, every-member ministry, the Kansas prophets, church planting, Willowcreek, Wimber, nurture courses, cell churches and so on.

But there are dangers in the current vogue for spirituality. As we saw in our examination of New Religious Movements in Chapter 2, some are merely the fashion of the moment which swoop across the scene leaving little behind. But there are others: most of these are ultimately 'religions of the self', concerned with the betterment of the individual. Others are foolish and some are dangerous. All of them absorb their followers and often crowd out any possibility of them responding to the love of God in the Christ who revealed that the Way was one of service and self-sacrifice, not one of self-fulfilment and self-gratification.

Renewals can be presented in various ways. Some invite other movements to come and join in an exploration, a voyage of discovery shared with others. Others are cut and dried and ask us to adopt them entire. The post-modern horror of the prepackaged suggests that the former approach will be more acceptable, as the success of Emmaus and Alpha suggests with their encouragement of discussion and participation.

One other thing is clear. With such a smorgasbord of possibilities and the limited attention span of many people it is not surprising that someone may be an enthusiastic adopter of one form of spirituality for a time, only to replace it with another a short while later. Indeed there is much anecdotal evidence that it is more common nowadays for those new church members who promised so well a few months back to be now nowhere to be seen. This may, of course, be due to the familiar temptations of the world, the flesh and the devil, but for many their 'Christian' phase will be seen as a significant but fleeting stage they passed through on their continuing journey.

Post-modernism is laid-back

Imagination, wit, laughter and the ability not to take anything too seriously are part of the post-modern approach. Anything which seems too intense or too demanding is discarded. A recent study of evangelists showed that the popular image of them as 'loud and insensitive, overintense, humourless and manipulative' was totally at odds with the way people today think about new ideas.[7] In today's climate that approach is likely to be counterproductive: it is not being faithful to God, it is being foolish.

Hence renewals which present themselves in dour manipulative terms will not grasp the attention. If they can laugh at the world and at themselves they will be given a hearing. This does not mean that they should not deal with serious matters, but they should have a light touch in presenting them.

This must include an inquiry into the being of God. The doctrine of the Holy Trinity speaks to post-modernists for it describes movement, relationship, paradox, co-operation and love – all familiar words in post-modern parlance. Indeed many Christians can learn from this, for too often we look to God for what we can get out of him – forgiveness, peace of mind, guidance – rather than to perceive who he is in all his transcendent immanence.

Post-modernists are allergic to the expert who stands and teaches, whether their subject matter is God or anything else. They have found that experts are often wrong, and they distrust those who claim a knowledge that puts them in a position of power which is too often misused. Post-modernists are prepared to probe alongside someone else, as can be seen in the proliferation of coaches and counsellors, but they are unwilling to be led, for they fear that they will be led by the nose. Hence those involved in renewal can approach others best through 'let's see where this leads us', rather than 'sit down and I will teach you all about it'.

Post-modernism distrusts logic but trusts experience

Since the progress beloved by modernism seems to post-modernists to have led to a science whose products they distrust intensely, whether it is genetically modified crops, BSE, nuclear power or government statements on food safety, they feel it has brought us into a mechanised wilderness which can do everything but value human behaviour and feelings. If knowledge is suspect then we have to rely on what we experience. The result is that human experience is too uncritically accepted, for we are in a credulous age. If someone claims to have been healed through aromatherapy or visited by aliens, their testimony will be listened to with attention and almost without question.

These are warm waters for renewals to swim in. We have already seen that renewals depend much upon the experience of individuals and that this emphasis can cloud the examination of the greater question: 'Does this experience reflect truth?' That question is anathema to post-modernists. They echo Nietzsche, who said, 'what therefore is truth? . . . truths are illusions of which one has forgotten that they are illusions; worn-out metaphors which have become powerless to affect the sense.'

Truth demands absolutes, and absolutes are unacceptable.

Therefore nothing is true and nothing is false: all is relative. Lesslie Newbigin noticed that Christians copy this when they say 'It seems to me' or 'I believe that . . .'. He comments: 'the language is generous and tolerant. But somewhere in it lurks the potential that all notions are held as true only "for me", with little or nothing presumed to be true also for others.'

The waters of experience which at first sight seem so favourable to renewals are therefore treacherous. They wash away all landmarks, and wreck the hopes of many who witness to Christ, for while people outside will give a courteous hearing to the stories of those involved in renewal, they will not follow the undeclared desire and embark on the same journey. Rather they will say, 'I'm glad that happened to you, but I am going this way . . .'. Since our experience of anything is unique to ourselves, others are under no obligation to follow us.

Further, because there are no absolutes and all things are relative, there are no boundaries – moral or otherwise. To say, 'adultery is wrong' or 'Christ is King', is to declare universal truths and both will be rejected. Thus if someone comes into the life of a renewal with this post-modern attitude they will have to learn the ethics of the Christian faith as well as its doctrine. Widespread amorality of this kind was last faced by the Church in the third and fourth centuries and their answer was the catechumenate – a two- or three-year preparation for baptism. At first reading these ancient training programmes are exceedingly moralistic, but with our own experience of the effect of amorality we can now see more easily how their teachers were trying to help the neophytes. New members of the Church needed help to think through the whole of their lives, so that the landmarks they had never had could be agreed and inculcated.

For this reason the methodology of the catechumenate is causing much interest at present and is expressed through such courses as 'Emmaus' and the Roman Catholic 'Rite for the Christian Initiation of Adults'. A more intimate approach to the same goal is seen in the growth of 'spiritual direction' in all traditions of the Church, though the word 'direction' is certainly not post-modernist.[8]

Post-modernism dismisses history

'Such has been the power and influence of the post-modernist critique of history that growing numbers of historians themselves are abandoning the search for truth, the belief in objectivity, and the quest for a scientific approach to the past.' This conclusion by Richard Evans[9] has three reasons. First, deconstructionism has meant a questioning of all historical reality: there is no such thing as a fact which has only one interpretation.[10] Secondly, the meta-narrative of reason and progress and the importance of power was central to modernist historians and this has been discarded. Thirdly, as John Vincent says, 'History is about winners, not losers . . . history is deeply male . . . history is about the rich and famous, not the poor'. The result is that: 'Nowadays we are far less confident about the "real facts" of history, and far less certain about where fact begins and fiction begins.'[11]

The Christian may have considerable sympathy with this approach, especially for the last reason. Post-modern historians tell the stories of the underdog, the servant, the women, the marginalised – just as the New Testament does. However, there are great dangers, for a renewal which forgets the tradition from which it emerges, can wander into a wasteland. The strongest renewals, as we have seen, are those which are either Strand B renewals which stay in contact with the mainstream or those Strand A renewals which reinterpret the tradition in the light of their new truth. Renewals which try to reinvent the Christian tradition are all too likely to end by not being Christian at all. There are many NRMs who have gone down that primrose path.

Post-modernism delights in the strange

The playful attitude beloved by post-modernism embraces satire and the frolic of a child. It delights in narrative, and the heart of many stories is the odd and the quirky. At times it seems that the offbeat is preferred to the ordinary simply because it is strange. But this is not confined to words: it also shows itself in life, where the exploration of the bizarre and the unusual can lead into dangerous territory. 'Learning to "lose yourself" can be an enlightenment, but it can also be strangely selfish: a greed for intense, ravishing experiences.'[12]

The downside of seeking the ever more outlandish is that it departs from one's real life which is often all too humdrum. Entering new experiences through drugs or addiction or meditation is perilous: it is, after all, only virtual reality – not reality itself. Too many renewals can betray themselves by concentrating on the unusual. Thus the modern charismatic movement has at times become overly fascinated by leg-lengthening, being 'slain in the Spirit', by 'words of knowledge' and by gold dentistry. The risk of this is that the real message of the renewal is clouded by the exceptional: once again we find the Devil's Distortion coming to pass – 'secondary matters to the centre'.

On the other hand, the post-modernist can teach us much about how to read the Bible with a greater understanding of how it was meant to be read. The modernist approach to hermeneutics is essentially logical: it examines a book like an ancient document and picks it to pieces. It takes a verse from here and a passage from there and, putting them together, defines or destroys a doctrine. Post-modernist hermeneutic is very different. It delights in its stories, its paradoxes, its sense of the importance of relationships, its mystery, its non-systematic approach, its non-powerful narrators, its humour, its multiple viewpoints,[13] its apocalyptic and its picture-language. The Bible which emerges may be more ambiguous and less clear-cut but it can be argued that it is truer to the original intention of the authors: it is certainly more enjoyable.

FUNDAMENTALISM

The twentieth century saw the rise of a conservative religious reaction which startled all those who had assumed that secularisation meant that religion would quietly retire to a rest home before its inevitable demise. Indeed, secularisation itself as propounded by the early sociologists has been questioned, some deriding it as itself being a 'faith', and others pointing out that it was a theory unsupported by facts.

'Fundamentalism' is a word best avoided since it has too many derogatory connotations, suggesting a closed and dangerous world associated with violence. But the conservatism of the American Bible Belt, and of Hasidic Judaism, Islamic Shari'a law and the Bharatiya Janata suggests that religion of that kind is growing, not declining. In part it is not difficult to see some of these movements as protests against the pervading Westernisation of the world. Their followers see their traditional culture as more moral, more protective and more religious than the Western culture they see on their television or which creeps into their shops and their work, and above all assails their young people. They want none of it. As Marty and Appleby see it, conservatism of this kind is a defence mechanism against the pressures of alien influences.[14]

One of the influences they are seeking to escape is the post-modernist approach to life outlined above. They see it as creating a society without ethical standards, recognising no sin (except intolerance) and recognising neither dark nor light. The difficulty is that the method they use to combat post-modernist relativism is a return to the scriptures which they hold to be sacred. And in doing so they often adopt a modernist approach which is logic-chopping, narrow and unimaginative. Thus Christians can lose the rainbow quality of the Bible in a whirl of words in which the living Word is lost. They retreat from what they perceive as a hostile post-modern world into a modernism which may be far more corrosive of faith.

Renewals do not have to embrace this thinking. Inevitably there are some who wish to retreat into the tradition, often into its strictest form so that they may keep the flame alive in what they perceive as its purest form. Other renewals, as we have seen, wish to escape from the apron strings of the past and create their own bright new world: for them the constrictions of 'fundamentalism' are clean contrary to the direction they are headed in. But the wise renewals are those which hold to the essence of the tradition and reinterpret it in the light of the discoveries they have made.

The present-day charismatic movement is in two minds about this. There are elements, especially those people who came out of the more conservative Protestant sects who wish to maintain an extremely precise doctrinal position. However there are others who relish the sense of space which they now enjoy and do not want to re-enter the ghetto. For many the ministry of women has been the touchstone – some resist any erosion of the concept of 'headship' while others are willing to open the doors of the Church as widely as possible.

The world around it sculpts a renewal. The two forces we have looked at in this chapter have to be taken into account for no renewal can fail to be influenced by its context. But at the end of the day the eternal human desire is still there:

> Encumbered forever by desire and ambition
> There's a hunger still unsatisfied
> Our weary eyes still stray to the horizon
> Though down this road we've been so many times.[15]

8 *The Hypothesis Reviewed*

We have traced the history of several renewals, and followed their often tortuous journeys. We have seen that the results of some of these apparently far-off events still reverberate, for all effective renewals create institutions – whether it is the format of the Christian Church left behind by the New Testament, the religious orders resulting from the decay of Cluny, the multifaceted modern implications of the Reformation or the evangelistic patterns flowing from the American Awakenings.

I have suggested that the courses which renewals follow are not purposeless meanderings but have a certain pattern, which I put forward as a hypothesis. By now you may have made up your mind on its validity. You may have found that it does not hold water and is best discarded. You may have found that it has the universal significance of a spiritual law. You may have found that it suggests a pattern which, although sometimes deviated from, is generally followed. For myself I would claim no more than the last statement, though I would also say that, if that is so, then we can learn much from it. I hope that the Conclusions which round off most chapters will have given some indications of the ways in which renewals develop and the opportunities and pitfalls that exist.

If the hypothesis stands up in most situations and in most contexts, then, in this final chapter, we need to summarise what are its implications. There are three possible scenarios:

1. Renewal in a local church
2. Renewal in a denomination
3. Renewal in the Church worldwide.

In particular we shall look at the different settings through the eyes of those who are called to leadership in that situation: it may be a local minister, a lay leader, the head of a diocese or district, a denominational leader or even the Pope himself. Renewals demand much of leaders for they disturb the waters.

RENEWAL IN A LOCAL CHURCH

In the 1970s I ministered in a church which experienced considerable charismatic renewal. However I found that this was not the first time that such renewal had taken place. In 1942 a curate had himself become involved with the Pentecostal movement; he had gathered a group around him and there had been considerable division. Part of the church, including the curate, joined a local Pentecostal church. The rawness of the wounds which had been caused were still present thirty years later and I well remember a very gracious leader in the church who came by himself most faithfully, while his wife went off to the Pentecostals as she had done since 1942. The interesting thing is the date: in 1942 any charismatic happenings were extraordinarily rare in mainline churches and, through inexperience, things may have been badly handled on both sides. I can imagine the excitement and exasperation on the part of those involved in the renewal and the bewilderment and antagonism of those who had never come across such a thing before. Possibly with more skilled leadership the split could have been avoided.

From the point of view of the leadership of a local church let us look at the different phases of a renewal that we have discerned.

Stage 1: Renewal

It may be that a few people from a church go to a Cursillo weekend, attend a charismatic conference, or come back rejoicing from a Celtic gathering. Often the initial impetus for renewal comes from outside a church, though it may be that a house group experiences something out of the ordinary which seems to them to have a touch of the Spirit. If a leader wishes to help a church into the direction of some sort of renewal it may well be right to encourage groups of people to go on something which is outside run-of-the-mill church activities – and this will often be outside the area served by the church. If, however, you are a leader who is not personally involved you may be faced by a group of people who have suddenly become excited and even ecstatic – and possibly erratic. They will find it very difficult to explain their feelings, and certainly will not yet be able to think about what has happened to them.

This is the period of experience, and experience is not best met by reason and by dismissive cold logic. The (mythical?) vicar who responded to the effervescence of the new Billy Graham convert by saying, 'Go to bed early – you'll feel better tomorrow', took the wrong tack. Experience is best met by humanity, by warmth of personal relationships, by seeking to find out what has happened and by enjoying some of the excitement of others. Above all it is necessary for leaders to sincerely seek what is the right path for themselves. If they are seen to be personally open to God's guiding then those in the renewal will be able to respect their leaders and therefore respond to them and learn from them.

Stage 2: Conflict

Too often renewals begin with battles. The wise leader will try to avoid confrontation. The pattern of Matthew 18:15–22 should be the norm for dealing with Christian disagreement: this commands that first of all there should be a private talk together, then, if the difficulty persists, a more formal but still confidential discussion between a small group. Only after that should the matter come to the notice of the church as a whole: 'megaphone diplomacy' is inappropriate and unscriptural.

The distinction between 'tension' and 'division' is important at this point. Tensions between those of different viewpoints are inevitable and even right. The New Testament itself is full of tensions – ecclesiastical, social, ethnic, doctrinal. From these tensions good things come. But divisions leading to one group leaving a church are very different. As we have seen in our examination of Strand A, those who divide from a church seldom prosper even on their own terms and all too often their action weakens the whole body of Christ.

If our hypothesis is right, one of the most important findings is that a Strand B renewal is preferable for the health of the whole church than a Strand A renewal and that this is true of local churches as well as the wider church.

Though it is disregarded by sociologists and considered to be an uncomfortable compromise by many, it seems to be Strand B which often does most to help the whole church. Strand A may sometimes lead to successful denominations but often at the cost of making the whole weaker. The same is true of a local church: division leading to the breaking of fellowship is something which can only be accepted after a situation becomes absolutely impossible, and, if there has been a break, the restoring of fellowship must be the highest priority. It is not for nothing that Paul uses a thesaurus of Greek words to urge unity on his churches – they are to be 'at one', 'knit together', 'harnessed together', 'attached' to each other, 'in harmony'. He was well aware of the many tensions which threatened the young churches and he did all in his power to keep them together. It is this that explains the unbridled and even vituper-ative language he uses towards those he saw as dividing the Church – whether they be the super-apostles of Corinth or the Judaisers we see scalded in his letter to the Galatians. However, it is Peter who puts the need for unity most succinctly:

> All of you, have unity of spirit, sympathy, love for one another, a tender heart, and a humble mind. Do not repay evil for evil or abuse for abuse: but on the contrary repay with a blessing.[1]

One of the most difficult issues in a local church is the

supposition that those involved in the renewal have had an experience which puts them on a higher spiritual plane than 'ordinary' Christians. Sometimes it is those directly associated with a renewal who make such claims and who urge others to climb up and join them. Sometimes they make no such assertion, but it is easy for others to feel that they are regarded as second-class. As we saw in Chapter 4, this 'spiritual elitism' is common. Leaders have the difficult task on the one hand of fostering humility on the part of those connected with the renewal – often by encouraging them to take a full part in the chores of the church – and on the other of helping those not involved to accept and listen to those who are.

The personal cost to the leader is considerable. Leaders who love and care for people will find that the tensions pierce their own heart. They feel for both – often longing to forward those elements within the renewal which are God-centred, and yet conscious of the negative reaction of others. On the other hand, leaders should not over-react. It is easy to feel the church is torn in two when really only a small minority are taking up positions on either side: it is often found that most people in a church continue as normal, unaware of the issues which are being so hotly debated by a minority. I have often found that leaders need to 'name the demons' – by listing those who are perceived to be causing difficulty – for it can feel as though the whole church is rent in two when the actual number involved is comparatively small. The leaders will often need to use the prayer: 'Grant us by the same Spirit to have a right judgement in all things'.[2]

Stage 3: Networking

The local renewal gathers pace. Some outsiders are attracted by the commitment and the excitement and the changed lives. Others are repelled. Despite their sometimes brash exterior those in the renewal are often uncertain of themselves, rightly feeling that they are venturing on a journey whose destination is precarious. As the sociologists have pointed out, they look both for respectability (a lowering of the boundaries) and for reinforcement of their belief. This is the time when church leaders may become uneasy when they find those in the renewal going to retreats and conferences, reading books and listening to tapes, meeting frequently with others involved and talking deep into the night. Leaders will fear that a 'holy huddle' is being formed: they may be right, but, as we have seen, networking is a necessary part of the progress of a renewal. Leaders must stay in touch, learn the jargon of the renewal so that they can talk the same language, and should not give any suggestion that they disapprove unless there are elements which are so sectarian that they have to be challenged. Leaders need to learn to bite their tongues.

It is here that the teaching ministry of the leader becomes significant. Those in the renewal need to hear how their experience fits into the whole structure of Christian faith. Their new ideas need to be fitted into the tradition both of spirituality and of doctrine. Incidentally, it is not helpful for the leader to say with a wry, world-weary smile, 'This has all happened before', and then cite the experience of the Cluniac monks or the Cane Ridge revivalists. As far as the renewalists are concerned their experience is sparklingly new. They may be glad to know that there are echoes in history, for renewals search for roots, but they do not want that information to be used to diminish their wondrous encounter with the living God.

Stage 4: Definition

Time passes. Renewal begins to become a way of life. The gatherings for fellowship become regular; the conduct of the meetings begins to develop a pattern. Sometimes, as in Cursillo, the meetings have an organised shape and expectation. At other times the unorganised becomes organised, as in the modern charismatic meetings – just as the new religious orders developed their routine and the Camp Meetings took a certain shape. A culture is born: certain things are done, often in a set order at predetermined times. This is inevitable, but the process can lead to a straitjacket: freedom produces conformity. This is often most obvious in the music and the teaching. Whether the music is plainsong, or Wesleyan hymns, or the latest charismatic choruses, renewals are often known by their singing: they have much to sing about and their music expresses their emotion. But what starts as precious and distinctive can in time harden into a required ritual. The 'time of worship' of the charismatic meeting becomes as formalised as evensong.

The same is true of preaching and teaching. Certain patterns of speech become hallowed by familiarity and come to be expected: certain phrases will elicit an 'Alleluia' from a Pentecostal church, and a Catholic sermon which does not include the word 'sacrament' will be deemed unsound. Even the length of the sermon becomes fixed: a thirty-minute sermon will seem interminable to many congregations, while others will find it woefully short. But this is not just a matter of words and form. In his preaching for conversion Finney expected certain consequences to follow in the lives of his hearers as a result of his words, just as a modern charismatic congregation is often expected to come for a 'time of ministry' after an effective sermon. Most involved in a renewal are eager for teaching, but they are also looking for words which rekindle the feelings they had at the time when the renewal was fresh and dynamic.

Stage 5: Divergence

If the culture which those interested in the renewal have come to recognise as theirs is not acknowledged in their local church, there is the real possibility of division. Some will feel that the teaching is inadequate, or that the worship does not give them an opportunity for expression, or that their enthusiasms cannot be contained in 'old wine-skins'. They may well reject their whole denomination: in the 1980s many in Britain shook the dust of their mainline churches off their feet in order to join the New Churches, believing that their former denominations were beyond redemption – and that the young, fresh churches they were joining were about to inherit the earth. Strand A flourished.

Those involved in the renewal therefore break fellowship and leave their old church. The pain for the leadership of their church is crippling. Those who leave have often been personally close, their contribution to the church invaluable, their spiritual life an inspiration. They may well have been people upon whom the leaders relied, and who had been helpers in many an initiative. In these painful situations there are three possible pitfalls for the leaders. First, they may decide that the whole renewal is too painful and its results too uncertain for it to be allowed to flourish, and so pull back from accepting the contribution it can make. Second, they may personally draw back from what it can offer to their own spiritual lives. Third, leaders can forget that, while some involved in the renewal have left, there are still others in the congregation, those who possibly had not previously said much and who had kept in the background during the time when disagreement was rife, but who still need the support and help of their church. Often they may be less forceful than those who have left and sometimes more stable: in the jargon, they are the 'late adopters' who think before they jump – but jump they have, often without telling anyone else. They are Strand B and they need pastoral care for they feel bewildered as they are torn in two directions.

If at all possible, though it may be at considerable personal cost, it is essential that those who are in Strand B should maintain friendship with those who have left, even if they themselves are classed as compromisers and fence-sitters by those in Strand A. Those who have left often find their new situation is not as helpful as they had anticipated and need friendship from outside. In particular, it is often found that the leadership in Strand A is not as dependable as had been expected and the transferees need help in working through their position. As we have seen, Strand B is important for the ultimate good both of Strand A and of the mainstream church, and those in Strand B should be shown that their halfway position is not a spineless, unimpressive refusal to make a decision, but has its own heroism and its own significance in the purposes of God for his whole Church. It is sad, whether in matters of faith, of personal relationships or of political life, when the word 'compromise' is seen as a word to be abhorred. Life with other human beings should always involve 'compassion, kindness, humility, meekness and patience'.[3]

Stage 6: Communication

The general experience when a group of people have broken away and formed their own church is that in the early years they keep themselves aloof from other Christians. In part this may be because of broken personal relationships, in part because they feel that their experience is exclusive to themselves, and in part they may be nervous because of the greater resources of the longer-established churches.

Time, however, introduces them to the reality of what life is like when a body of human beings work together: relationships break and need repairing; some individuals need much pastoral care; crises occur and need to be dealt with; the leadership is not appreciated by everyone. The problems faced by St Paul are still with us. Further, all the things which the group thought they had thankfully left behind re-emerge – fund-raising, the upkeep of buildings, administration. If the church grows, all the issues surrounding institutionalisation and bureaucratisation become urgent – and if not dealt with become fatal. The result is that the new group realises that they have more in common with other churches than they had at first thought and they may well start joining with other church leaders for prayer, or coming tentatively to ecumenical events. It has been possible to see this in the evolution of the New Churches in recent years as most of them have become part of the wider church scene. The leaders of the new group should be prepared to take this step, despite the misgivings which some of their church members may have.

It is here that those Strand B people still in their mainstream churches can play an indispensable role both in welcoming the newcomers and in explaining to those in the other churches what their distinctive viewpoint is. Church leaders should encourage Strand B in every way they can to act as go-between, learning from them the best way to help the Strand A group enter fully into Christian fellowship and work with the other churches.

Stage 7: Consequences

We have set out the possibilities in Chapter 1 – fragmentation, the formation of a new denomination or assimilation.

For a Strand A church, fragmentation is an ever-present threat. Because the group have split from one church it makes it easier for another schism to take place when difficulties arise – just as couples with one divorce behind them are statistically more likely to divorce again. Often the original split may well have been led by someone whom Weber would say had a 'charismatic' personality. When this person becomes the leader of their 'own' church difficulties are likely to occur as their strong style, which at first seemed so masterful, begins to appear domineering or manipulative. Only if some form of collaborative leadership emerges can this danger be avoided – but along with that can come the paraphernalia of elections, committees and politics, which are often the very things the church has been set up to avoid. It is not an easy conundrum to solve, and many churches have fragmented into nothingness because of it.

However, if the church survives its infancy and grows it may come in time to plant new churches and become a new small denomination. At that stage it will have to face the necessary growth of bureaucratisation that goes with it. To get to this stage demands outstanding leadership, for the church needs to be expanded from a small gathering of the like-minded to a considerable organisation; few people have both the pastoral and teaching skills so necessary in the early days and also the administrative expertise demanded as the church grows. It is usually because of questions of leadership that so few break-away churches grow permanently beyond fifty or sixty people.

The third possibility is assimilation. Sometimes the new church fails, its numbers drop and the bright freshness degenerates into a dull routine. Members drift back to the church they left – or, more usually, because of the personal factors of hurt and pride, to another mainline church. Eventually the church drifts into dissolution – usually with more of a whimper than a bang.

RENEWAL IN A DENOMINATION

When the Gentile Church came into being the Jewish leaders were disturbed; Cluny's growth frightened the local bishops; the Reformation threw the Vatican into turmoil; the Awakenings turned the American Church upside down. In more modern times the waves of renewal which have swept over the Church have led to condemnatory motions in synods and presbyteries,[4] perplexed faces among bishops and denominational leaders and much uncertainty as to how they are to be handled.

Let us look at the matter from the point of view of a denominational leader.

Stage 1: Renewal

One thing is often overlooked. If someone is upset about a matter in the Church they write a 'something ought to be done about it' letter to the bishop or put down a hostile motion at a synod. Therefore the first that church leaders may hear about a renewal is likely to be negative. It is difficult for them to overcome this initial view, which may prejudice them for some time. This is particularly true if those concerned in the renewal do not tell their leaders what is happening, or if the only stories they can tell are breathless and euphoric descriptions of their experience.

In virtually all denominations church leaders are supposed

to be responsible for right teaching. It is therefore inevitable that they are cautious when faced with people who claim to have had an apparition of the Virgin Mary, or who say they have received new charismatic gifts or that they have a vision which has 'led' them to a certain course of action. Much misunderstanding is caused by this: those in the renewal feel their leaders should immediately and joyfully adopt their own viewpoint, not realising that the leader has many issues to consider. However, the renewalists often have a case: caution in a church leader is right up to a point, but not when it leads to the paralysis of indecision. Indeed, leaders may be too often appointed to their posts because they are guarded and reticent people rather than risk-taking and adventurous – selecting a 'fence-sitter' stirs up no dust.

Wise leaders always want to see for themselves. Nicodemus is often castigated for coming to Jesus 'by night' as though he was a coward because he did not come more openly – but in fact it was the sensible action of a responsible leader. He had heard much about Jesus, both good and bad: now he rightly wanted to find out at first hand. Merely going and hearing Jesus speak in public would not give him an opportunity to find out the full facts, so he came when it was possible to talk face to face. Despite, or because of, the fact that Jesus bewildered and challenged him he was not put off – even when Jesus pulled his leg ('Are you a teacher of Israel, and yet you do not understand these things?'). His sincerity of purpose is shown by his reaction to the incident. We see his courage in his acceptance of the mockery of the Pharisees, and his generosity in the immense quantity of spices he brought to the tomb for the embalming of Jesus.[5]

Nicodemus showed the sensible shrewdness of a good leader and yet a willingness to become involved personally if in fact his investigations showed that the 'Jesus movement' was of God. The great scholar Gamaliel showed a commendable fair-mindedness which stemmed the rush to condemn the followers of Jesus, but apparently he did not follow that by a personal quest.[6] It is Nicodemus who is the better example to the

Christian leader when he or she is told of a rustling of a wind of the Spirit which appears to have no history (John 3:8).

The opportunities for misunderstanding at this phase are considerable. Both the leaders of the church and those involved in the renewal come from different viewpoints. The former want to see if there is reality behind the renewal, and judge it by its effect on people and by its scriptural validity. Those in the renewal can only judge by the overwhelming experience they have had. Therefore the church leaders can seem stuffy and overcautious, while those in the renewal can sometimes not hear the criticisms of others – even when they are justified. We encountered, for example the hurt response of Abbot Peter to St Bernard's vigorous criticisms. Those in love are often oblivious to the most glaring faults in their beloved: it is the same with renewals. Those outside can often be the wisest guide. Unfortunately those inside often do not want to hear, interpreting even the friendliest comments as an attack.

Nevertheless the importance of an outside reference point for those involved in renewals cannot be overstated. Whether it is a spiritual director, a respected Christian friend, or a group of advisers, the thoughtful view from outside can be of greatest value. It was for this reason that the New Churches soon discovered that they had a need for an 'apostle' who could give 'extra-local' leadership.

Stage 2: Conflict

Denominational leaders will inevitably find themselves drawn into adjudicating between those involved in the renewal and those outside. Sometimes this is a conflict within a church which they are called upon to settle. More significantly, there may well be wider conflicts.

As we have seen, one of the main conflicts in America was theological. The conservatism of the frontier did not chime well with the prevailing eastern viewpoint which owed so much to the semi-Christianity of Arius and the deistic anti-clericalism of Tom Paine. The contemporary church leaders, living in the atmosphere of the eastern seaboard, found what they considered the raw-boned simplistic slogans of the revivalists alarming and dangerous. There was no meeting of minds and the result was schism. If the leaders of the mainline churches had been able to show that they understood and, to some extent accepted, the revivals, there might be fewer denominations in the United States today.

The handling of the East African revival, which has been continuing through many phases since the 1930s, shows a better approach. The bishops and other leaders were initially alarmed by this outbreak of revival and by such practices as the open confession of sins and an aggressive (though cheerful) evangelism. However, they remained in close contact with those in the revival and many of the leaders were personally deeply affected by it. One of my own friends was a missionary in Central Africa in the late 1950s and in humility she had knelt before the Africans she had gone to teach and asked them to lay hands on her and pray that she might receive what they had received. The result has been a church of infectious enthusiasm and mature leadership, which has been able to endure the years of war and the political and economic turmoil which has engulfed all too much of that part of Africa.

Being a denominational leader in such circumstances requires much grace. It is not easy to listen to the enthusiasms of others and not feel personally threatened. It is not easy to understand a very different viewpoint from one's own. It is not easy to accept with a wry smile the unjust accusations of being someone who is overly circumspect and motivated by church politics.

There are also times when the discipline inherent in leadership has to be exercised. It is wise not to be too meticulous about infringements of church order, for enthusiasm often leaps over what it sees as petty rules concerning liturgy and church government. Indeed it is the challenge that a renewal presents which can often clear out the fusty remains of yesterday. The Church of England's official prayers and pattern of ministry have been considerably influenced by the effects of the charismatic movement and by such renewals as Cursillo and Focalare.

At the same time the leader will encounter all too often a misuse of power. We have seen how this has distorted renewals from the New Testament itself down to the present day. On this the church leadership should be firm and decisive. Too often those involved in a renewal do not see clearly what is happening, and they can be manipulated and harmed all too easily. It is part of the function of the denominational leaders to exercise a right discipline within the Church of God.

Above all, renewal demands much pastoral care from church leaders in helping hurt congregations and people who have been bruised by the renewal. Sadly, most renewals leave behind them a distressing trail of casualties. The main army has gone on but the wounded remain behind, and often it is left to the church leaders to pick them up and give them succour.

Stage 3: Networking

Denominational leaders are often asked to spread a mantle of respectability over a renewal. As we have seen, renewals have a desire to find roots and acceptance. If a bishop or the President of the Methodist Conference or someone of similar status attends a renewal conference, says a word of encouragement, or writes an article bestowing legitimacy upon the movement, it is eagerly welcomed. This is the time of networking, of the great conference, and of working out what the renewal really stands for. If those in the movement receive help in this from their church leaders it will be seen as having great significance.

My own predecessor as Bishop of Pontefract was Richard Hare; for many years he was the only Church of England bishop who was prepared to be personally associated with the charismatic renewal. His open stance gave great encouragement to many charismatics, for it showed that they were not forgotten and that they had a voice in the church hierarchy. His presence and his teaching at the networking conferences kept many Anglicans in their churches when there was considerable pressure to leave and join the New Churches which were springing up all over Britain, promising freedom in the Spirit and much else. This Strand B within the Church of England was to provide many of its prospective leaders and profoundly influence its future.

Stage 4: Definition

As the years pass, the theological and ecclesiological issues come to the fore. What makes this renewal different from what has gone before? What sort of church is emerging from the renewal? What pattern of church governance is appropriate? What is its stance on mission?

The Reformation is an example we have looked at. The great theologians of the Reformation rewrote the textbooks of Christian theology, but in such a way as to combine the traditional with their new insights. The importance of this period in a renewal can be all too well seen in their handling of the mission of the Church. Because of what we can now see was a mistake, their territorial ecclesiology held up the evangelisation of the world for generations.

It is here that the denominational leaders can contribute much. First, they can encourage the renewal to think of itself in relation to the whole of the Christian faith. Thus Tom Smail one of the leaders of charismatic renewal in England, was challenged to draw the attention of the renewal to the person of God the Father. The result was his book *The Forgotten Father*, which encouraged the charismatic movement to look more deeply at the whole being of the Trinity and not to be solely preoccupied with the Holy Spirit.[7]

Secondly, leaders can ask the right questions. Renewals are too often guided by fashion and occasionally need a jolt. Bandwagons always need to be carefully examined to see if their contents are wholesome. Issues can be avoided and hard questions ducked, and it is the role of the leader to pose them. Archbishop Runcie told the evangelical movement in England in the 1980s that they should critically examine their ecclesiology: he was right to do so, and it led to a fruitful switch in evangelical thinking.

Thirdly, leaders should talk theologically with those in the renewal. Books and articles are good up to a point but it is in face-to-face discussion that people engage as people as well as proponents of certain viewpoints. Denominational leaders are often in the position to be able to set up such dialogue and they should do so whenever appropriate.

Stage 5: Divergence and Stage 6: Communication

The denominational leader will often treat these two stages together since his or her task is to keep lines of communication open when a rift has occurred.

If splits occur within a church it may well be easier for the denominational leader to be able to handle it with under-standing than for the local church leaders, who are too personally bewildered and hurt. Because they can maintain a certain distance denominational leaders can, with integrity, wish those who leave well, even though they will want to say that they regret their action. Similarly they are able to invite the leaders of the breakaway church to ecumenical events and show an interest in their welfare and this may begin the process of communication, which may have beneficial results in the future.

The denominational leader will want, in nearly every case, to remind those in the local churches that those who have diverged from their fellowship are still sisters and brothers in Christ and to be treated as such. They are therefore to be welcomed whenever possible and overtures should be made to them, even if initially these are apparently disregarded. Many ecumenical leaders will remember ruefully the 'seventy times seven' approaches which have been made unsuccessfully to a church and the joy with which they have received at last some hesitant response.

Stage 7: Consequences

The denominational leader will wish to commiserate with (and possibly welcome back) those in Strand A who have found that the grass was not greener on the other side and whose new fellowship has broken up or fizzled out. If, however, the new church has grown into a new denomination then it is of the greatest importance that the leaders of that church should be involved in prayer and planning for the good of the whole Church. I remember with great thanksgiving the preparations for the Decade of Evangelism when I was able to sit down to think about the evangelisation of England with leaders from the Roman Catholic Church as well as the New Churches. For many of the latter it was the first time they had been consulted and their views respected, and they found it both refreshing and an enlargement of their horizons, as did the rest of us as we gained from their input.

However, it is with Strand B, still directly in their care, that the denominational leaders will have most to do. Some ministers may be part of the renewal, and so will many of the laity. Many English bishops have been startled to see charismatic hands raised in worship during an apparently straightforward diocesan service. Their ministry to these people is important for Strand B has much to offer to the church – an understanding of the renewal and all that it has come to mean to them and also a loyalty to their own denomination. Leaders should listen to them, come to understand and value them, and then be prepared to learn from them. Very often they are the most active people in their churches and the most generous in their financial giving. A leader has to rise above his or her own limitations of spiritual and theological understanding to embrace with warmth these who have so much to bring.

RENEWAL IN THE WORLDWIDE CHURCH

As we look back on the history of renewals certain things are clear. First, renewals are part of the lifeblood of the Church. It was born in a renewal and the periodic refreshings of the Holy Spirit have been vital both for its inner life of prayer and worship and for its mission in the world. We have looked at four renewals in history and thought about the contemporary scene. Despite all the failings which we are able to perceive with the benefit of hindsight, the Church would be poorer without the Gentile Church, and without the Cluniac renewal, the Reformation and the American Awakenings. The same is true today for the Church would be less robust, less prayerful – and infinitely less interesting – without the insights of the charismatics, the 'Celts', the Cursillistas and the others involved in various forms of renewal. If that is true of the developed world it is infinitely more significant in the Church in the two-thirds world, for these different movements of the Holy Spirit have strengthened Christians under pressure, given them a gospel to die for and helped the churches there to expand exponentially.

Secondly, our journey through history suggests that what we have called Strand B is of great significance. Too often overlooked, it is those in Strand B who have commonly been the foundation for what has lasted in the church.

Thirdly, while renewals are a mixture of all too much of human nature with all too little of the Spirit, the reality of the work of God cannot be denied. Whether it is the development of the gospel into a world-claiming faith, or the expansion of the Church through the religious orders or through more modern evangelistic campaigns, God has been present to bring healing to his world. When we cut away the ballyhoo and the hyperbole and the exaggerated claims, there is a massive residue which speaks of the genuine action of the Holy Spirit.

9 Does the Splendour Have to Fade?

The title of this book is taken from the Revised Standard Version of 2 Corinthians 3:12,13 where the descent of Moses from Mount Sinai is used as an example to contrast the hope in the law and the hope in Christ:

> Since we have such a hope, we are very bold, not like Moses, who put a veil over his face so that the Israelites might not see the end of the fading splendour.

However, the title ends with a question mark, which is not in the quotation. Must all invigorations of the Holy Spirit end in ordinariness? As we asked in the Introduction, 'Why do cups of tea always become lukewarm?'

We have traced the history of several renewals and have to admit that we appear to have seen a 'fading splendour' in each case. The ardour of the New Testament was not maintained into the second century; Cluny degenerated; the Reformation did not deliver all it promised; the American Awakenings lost their vigour. And it has to be said that there are many involved in modern renewals of one kind or another who find that their thrill does not seem to last for ever: the New Churches have not converted the land, Cursillo is helpful just to a few and the 'Celts' resonate only with some. Is this inevitable – and if so, what do we do about it?

IS IT INEVITABLE?

I think that, from our examination of the facts, we have to accept that renewals inevitably change and appear to lose their intensity. We have looked at various things which sap the energy of a renewal – possessions, prayerlessness, division, inadequate leadership and so on. But even when all that is taken into account there seems almost to be a spiritual requirement that renewals will change and lose their focus. I can only suggest most tentatively various reasons why this should be so.

Renewals affect individuals

This means that our usual personal dynamics come into play. We suffer from laziness and the inability to concentrate on one thing for any length of time; we feel overwhelmed by the pressures of life and the need to earn our daily bread. For many people it is the humdrum nature of everyday life which crowds out the glory of God. For a few in this post-modern world renewal is something taken up and then discarded like a new toy, but there are far more 'who are choked by the cares and riches and pleasures of life, and so their fruit does not mature'.[1]

But that same Parable of the Sower can give us a lead into the effect of renewal in the life of the individual. The seed of renewal is sown – but then it has to germinate and grow. And in the process of growth it changes: as Paul says in talking of the resurrection of the body at death, 'you do not sow the body that is to be, but a bare grain, perhaps of wheat or of some other grain'.[2] The same is true of renewal. Its effect in the human life inevitably changes with time – indeed an attempt nostalgically to recover the 'bare grain' of the original experience is doomed to failure. We have to move on, for we are pilgrims seeking a goal not tourists revisiting the ruined sites of the past.

Further, the grain may fall in better soil than we expect. The biblical view of growth is that it is both gradual and mysterious. The result of renewal may be different from what we expect, but it may still be 'a hundredfold, some sixty, some thirty' as it affects our lives and through us the lives of others. Some time ago I preached in a rural church at their harvest festival.

Afterwards we had a magnificent country meal, and I happened to be sitting next to a farmer. Having preached from the Parable of the Sower, I asked him, 'If you sow a bushel of wheat how many bushels do you expect to get in return?' He replied, 'Oh, in a really good year we might get fifty bushels, but it is usually thirty-five to forty.' In Jesus' day, as in the two-thirds world today, the thought of thirtyfold, let alone a hundredfold was beyond their imagining. Jesus' story would have been greeted with a guffaw of ridicule – as he intended, for he often used exaggeration to drive home his point. So it is with us: our 'bare grain' can often yield far more than we expect, mysteriously and unexpectedly and wonderfully.

Renewals affect groups of people

We looked at some of the sociological evidence because socio-logists can tell us something of how we interact and and how we react to different situations. From the very beginning of Christianity, the Church has been with us, whether we like it or not. The Christian faith is essentially communal and so the Church is part of the foundation of the faith. And groups of people, even if they are involved in renewal, can often behave foolishly and sinfully. Indeed, their own commitment to the renewal can blind them to deficiencies obvious to outsiders.

For this reason a renewal inevitably changes as the com-munity alters and either grows or diminishes. But a renewal does change the Church. As we have seen, it brings life where it was moribund and freshness where there was fustiness. Renewals are necessary for its well-being.

Renewals exist in the real world

Renewals often seek to change the world and too often end with the world changing them. This is not necessarily wrong, for the interplay between the Church and its context is part of the bringing in of the Kingdom of God, despite the messy compromises that that involves. Even a Carthusian monk has to live in the world: complete withdrawal is not an option, for even St Simon Stylites found that his pillar did not separate him from the people who came to receive counsel, and to bring him food.[3]

We therefore have to conclude that renewals are bound to change and that their energy levels are bound to become lower.

WHAT DO WE DO ABOUT IT?

Our second question is harder. It is seldom sensible to fight against reality, for sooner or later it rebounds vindictively. Castles in the sky hurt people when they fall. It is therefore no good trying to pretend that in the Christian world our humanity is different from those around us. We may have entered into the 'new creation' but we are still human beings with all the usual temptations and limitations. Playing 'Let's pretend' is not an option, whether this is thinking that the usual temptations of money, power and sex do not affect us or that a Christian fellowship is immune from the ills which afflict every other human organisation.

Nor should we overspiritualise the matter and leave God to sort out our problems. The last on the list of the 'fruit of the Spirit' in Galatians 5:22,23 is the word *enkrateia*, which is often translated as 'self-control', but which can probably be better rendered as 'taking responsibility for oneself'. Renewals begin in prayer and, if all is well, are borne along by prayer, but that does not absolve us from taking responsibility for our actions, even if we claim that they are under the guidance of the Holy Spirit.

Finally, we should see things through God's eyes. Was the decay of Cluny entirely a bad thing? It meant that a sprawling ecclesiastical empire was replaced by several fleet-footed, flexible religious orders with great potential for the future. The change from the camp meeting to the modern evangelistic organisations produced something which was suitable for a much wider context than the plains of the western United

States, even if it may be thought that the systematisation brought a narrowing of its focus.

The conclusion has to be that it is best not to fight the changes which take place in renewal movements with the passage of time. They have their different phases and these are not to be resisted but to be worked with. Thus:

- Church leaders, both local and denominational, should check any attempt to return on a nostalgia trip to the initial renewal: the eyes of congregations and denominations should be kept looking forward rather than backward.[4]
- The bureaucratisation of the renewal should not be resisted but done as efficiently as possible.
- There should be a widening of horizons from the object of the initial renewal – whether it be 'Baptism in the Spirit', Benedictine purity or justification by grace through faith – to encompass the whole of the Christian faith.

Above all there should be no lessening of God-centredness: some of the initial fervour may become cooler, but the continual standing on tiptoe waiting for the action of God in the future must be not be diminished and the 'still, small voice' must not be muffled.

The stream started high in the mountains and tumbled freshly and freely down the steep slope, little more than a rivulet at first and then gaining strength from a myriad of trickles. But as it reached the bottom of the mountain it slowed, became heavy with the mud it had washed down, and eventually meandered apparently purposelessly across the plain. But from time to time a tributary would flow into the river, and it was fresh and invigorating and below its junction with the river the fish flourished and the reeds grew tall. But after a time the river returned to its turbid self, until another tributary entered and once again it felt rejuvenated. And there was a purpose behind it all, for in the end it entered the boundless sea of the love of God: the Bride had come to her Bridegroom.

Notes

Introduction

1. Philip Richter and Leslie Francis, *Gone but not Forgotten* (DLT, 1998).
2. Paul Tillich, *The Recovery of the Prophetic Tradition* (1950). N.B. Tillich is using the words 'sect' and 'church' in the technical sociological sense that will be examined later.
3. David Jones, 'A, a, a, Domine Deus' in *The Sleeping Lord and other Fragments* (1974).
4. David J. Bosch, *Transforming Mission* (1991).
5. In *The Structure of Scientific Revolutions* (1962) Kuhn defined a paradigm as, 'the entire constellation of beliefs, values, techniques, and so on shared by members of a given community'. He also made the point that a new paradigm can only be understood by those who are committed to it, 'one can only accept a paradigm's validity if one has stepped into its circle'. This lack of understanding and the consequent bewilderment of those who do not belong to the new way of thinking is not confined to scientific history – we shall meet it often in this book.
6. Paul Hiebert, *Epistomological foundations for Science and Theology* (1985).
7. In *Mind the Gap – some Reflections on Mission* (n.d.).
8. In some cases lack of finance can be a major factor. The lack of money in the Church of England in the early 1990s forced radical questions to be asked. The Evangelical Church in Germany is presently having to ask the same questions for the same reason.
9. Revival can mean no more than a series of meetings. I once saw outside an American Church, 'There will be a Revival here from October 15th through 25th'. We shall not use 'revival' in this book in this way, except in Chapter 6 which deals with American Awakenings.
10. Loisy's cynical comment, 'Jesus foretold the Kingdom and it was the Church which came', deserves critical examination. They are not automatic opposites.
11. 'Revitalisation Movements', *American Anthropologist* (1955).
12. The word 'sect' is used here and throughout the book in its sociological sense: i.e. as merely descriptive of a form of organisation. In normal speech it is often derogatory, carrying the sense of exclusivity. It is not being used in this looser sense here or elsewhere (except in quotations). The word is examined more closely in Chapter 2.
13. The House Churches are now more accurately described as New Churches – many have long since outgrown their beginnings in private houses. They will be called by the latter name in this book.
14. Discernment (*diakrisis*) means 'making a distinction' or 'appraisal'. In 1

Cor.12:10 it is used about discerning good and evil spirits, but it is not confined to that: Heb. 5:14 uses it in a more general sense.

15. Acts 6:7.
16. E.g. Jeremiah 14:13–16.
17. Matthew 21:11 and also 13:57; Mark 6:15; Luke 7:16; 24:19; John 4:19; 9:17.
18. Hebrews 10:11f. The whole argument of chapters 2–10 is centred on this theme.
19. Cf. Jeremiah 1:10. The call to be both priest and prophet (along with the requirement of celibacy) made Jeremiah's task harder and led to the intense internal struggle which he records in 1:4–19; 11:18–12:13; 15:10–16:4; 20:7–18.
20. Isaiah 6:6.
21. *Mind the Gap.*
22. Matthew 26:73.
23. Cf. Luke 21:5. Their awestruck 'Look at that!' is the cry of the archetypal tourist.
24. John 11:50.
25. Marx's over-used phrase about religion being the 'opium of the people' deserves to be put in its full context. He said, 'Religion is the sigh of the oppressed creature, the heart of a heartless world, and the soul of soulless conditions. It is the opium of the people.'
26. John T. Finney, *Recovering the Past* (1996).
27. The diversity and number of these can be seen most easily in the *UK Christian Handbook* where the list covers many pages – and that is only the UK! It has to be said that the *Handbook* also illustrates how many overlap with the work of others, with consequent waste of resources.
28. Bosch, *Transforming Mission.*
29. Karl Barth, *Evangelical Theology: an Introduction* (1963).
30. Karl Rahner, *Theological Investigations* (1972).

CHAPTER 1: *Hypothesis*

1. Cf. William Glen (ed.), *The Mass-Extinction Debates: How Science works in a Crisis* (1994). Cf. also K.T. Thomson, *Anatomy of the Extinction Debate* (1988). The reception of the continental drift theory is discussed in *The Road to Jaramillo* (1982).
2. Acts 11:18. The importance of this realisation is shown by the space given in Acts to the Cornelius story and its consequences, not least in the Synod of Jerusalem.
3. Andrew Walker, *Restoring the Kingdom* (1985) argues that the Catholic Apostolic Church was also part of the roots of the New Church movement.
4. Richard F. Lovelace, *Dynamics of Spiritual Life* (1979).
5. Wayne Meeks, *The First Urban Christians* (1983).
6. The weight which is to be given to the 'prophetic' writings of Ellen White and the reality of the 'Heavenly Sanctuary' said to have been founded in 1844 is of great importance to the future of the movement, which is deeply divided on the issue.
7. Romans 6:1.
8. Robert Burns mercilessly lampooned this narrowness: e.g. in 'Holy Willie's Prayer':

> Lord, hear my earnest cry and prayer
> Against the Presbytry of Ayr.

9. The Levellers, under the uncertain leadership of John Lilburne, sought, in the seventeenth century, a democracy that was not attained until the nine-

teenth – universal male suffrage, elected judges, and, above all, the opportunity for anyone to advance through their own merits rather than by birth or wealth. They were powerful in the 1640s but almost extinct by 1660.

10. This is a quotation from Numbers 10:29 where Moses invites his father-in-law to accompany them into the desert. It was not entirely appropriate since Hobab says 'No'!

11. Thus the charismatic movement in the UK deliberately sought dialogue with non-charismatic evangelicals in 1975. This led to the publication of the Report 'Gospel and Spirit' (1977). In the same way a series of discussions between charismatics and the World Council of Churches begain in 1978: the results were published in *The Church is Charismatic* (1981).

12. *The Charismatic Movement in the Church of England* (1981): italics in the original.

CHAPTER 2: *Sociology and All That*

1. Philip E. Hammond (ed.), *The Sacred in a Secular Age* (1985).

2. New Religious Movements (NRMs) cover a wide variety of beliefs. Note however that: not all are new – the Book of Mormon was published in 1830; not all of them are outwardly religious – some forms of therapy claim to be based on scientific fact; nor are all of them Movements – with all that that implies of organisation and direction. Nevertheless, despite its deficiencies NRM is a useful cover-all, non-judgemental name which covers many thousands of unrelated groups. This book does not use the word 'cult' which is derogatory: besides, 'one person's cult is another person's faith'.

3. Luke 16:15.

4. Sorokin died in 1968. He was head of the department of sociology at Harvard. His eclectic interests can be gauged from his founding of a research centre 'devoted to the study of the saints of the past, of educational theories for moral transformation and of ego-transcending techniques'.

5. Thus Sorokin, in *Sociocultural Causality, Space, Time*, says that even in the US 'different religious, occupational, economic, national and cultural groups . . . have different rhythms and pulsations, and therefore different calenders and different conventions for the sociocultural time of the groups'. Useful questions to any group are, 'How many have a diary?', 'Do you wear a watch?'.

6. John A. Saliba, *New Religious Movements* (1995).

7. In Islam also the community is of the greatest importance and it is seen as a way of life rather than belief in a creed. However there is, in the first of the Pillars, a credal statement: 'There is no god but God and Muhammad is the apostle of God'.

8. Cf. Malcolm Rue, 'Christians as Believers', in *Religious Organisation and Religious Experience*, ed. J. Davis (1982).

9. C.S. Lewis, *The Four Loves* (1960).

10. Jim Kiernan, *Authority and Enthusiasm* (1982). Zulu Zionism was founded in 1904 as an unusual combination of Dutch Reformed authoritarianism and Pentecostal freedom.

11. Richard F. Lovelace, *Dynamics of Spiritual Life* (1979).

12. Kant (1724–1804) encountered the fanatical German *Schwarmerei*. This influenced his 'critical' view of religion which demanded 'a critique of all theology': cf. Ronald Knox, *Enthusiasm* (1950).

13. Note how Paul uses personal testimony at the tense synod in Jerusalem: Acts 15:12.
14. Another reaction to prophecy is given in the Zulu Zion Churches where prophets 'are not noted for their self-restraint and are frequently likened to children for their irresponsibility'.
15. Roger Finke and Rodney Stark, *The Churching of America 1776–1990* (1992).
16. Bryan Wilson, *Sects and Society* (1961). Cf. also his *Patterns of Sectarianism* (1967) and *Religious Sects* (1970).
17. Politicians have also picked up this usage: e.g. 'We are a broad church party'.
18. Max Weber, *Economy and Society* (1978).
19. Sometimes this group is given a semi-official position as an 'eldership'. The possibilities of conflict between this group and legal church committees is considerable. The same rivalry can be seen in 10 Downing Street between the 'Kitchen Cabinet' of unelected advisers brought in by the Prime Minister and the official Cabinet answerable to Parliament.
20. The word 'routinisation' is that used by Weber. It is very similar to the 'institutionalisation' which other authors use.
21. Max Weber, *The Social Psychology of the World Religions* (1946).
22. Except perhaps by force. The Communist sect in China had, by the 1960s become 'church'. Mao deliberately tried to turn it back to being a sect through the Cultural Revolution: the dislocation and deaths involved showed the near-impossibility of resisting this process.
23. Weber, *Economy and Society*.
24. James Burchaell, *From Synagogue to Church* (1992).
25. In 1963 Benton Johnson preferred a continuum which showed the 'degree of tension between a religious group and its sociocultural environment'. Sects are high tension, churches low tension. This may well be a more accurate viewpoint than Weber's either/or diagnosis.
26. The curse against heretics was set out in the Eighteen Benedictions published at Jamnia c.AD 85: 'and may the Nazarenes and the heretics (*minim*) perish quickly'. It was an almost inevitable closing of the boundary in the wake of the destruction of the Temple in AD 70.
27. These racial elements were evident in Seymour's clash with Charles Parham, who had had some previous connections with the Ku Klux Klan. One of Parham's criticisms of Seymour's services was that people 'crowded around the altar like hogs, black and white mingling'.
28. Steve Bruce, *God Save Ulster* (1986).
29. Finke and Stark, *The Churching of America*.
30. This is a factor in a number of Islamic communities in the UK at present.
31. Blake's poem 'Jerusalem' is a good example of the standard Non-conformist Protestant belief in Joseph's visit accompanied by Christ. Hence 'And did those feet in ancient times . . .'. The answer to the questions in the first four lines is in each case, 'No'.
32. Peter Berger and Thomas Luckmann, *The Social Constriction of Reality* (1966).
33. Even among New Churches this takes place. According to *The Body Book* (1996) 6% fewer adults attended in 1996 compared to 1995 – the first decline recorded.
34. Carl Dudley, *Where Have All Our People Gone?* (1979).
35. Mark 11:28.
36. Recent scholarship now thinks it was unlikely that the Jewish synod of Jamnia, where Jewish teachers gathered to form some sort of succession to

the Sanhedrin, set the Old Testament canon, but no further books were admitted afterwards.

37. Clifford Geertz, *Religion as a Cultural System* (1966).
38. 1 Corinthians 1:26.
39. Thus the Alamo Christian Foundation declined sharply when Susan Alamo died (she was kept unburied for a time, waiting for a miraculous resurrection).
40. L. Festinger, H. W. Rueken and S. Schachter, *When Prophecy Fails* (1956).
41. Though this was only 2% of the membership.
42. Barbara Harrison, *Visions of Glory* (1978).
43. Peter Berger, *The Social Reality of Religion* (1973).
44. Martin Hubback, *The Prophets of Doom: the Security of Religious Cults* (1996). It is a report published by the Institute for European Defence and Strategic Studies, an independent think-tank.
45. This was the twelfth and most serious attack by the Aum Shinrikyo. They were well funded and had a laboratory with many scientists exploring means of mass destruction. Only technical problems connected with delivering poison gas prevented an even worse catastrophe.
46. According to their literature a 'Falun' is 'an intelligent spinning body of high energy pulsating in the inner abdomen of the practitioner', which imparts 'highly classified knowledge'.
47. For example, the gurus of Transcendental Meditation.
48. Phillip E. Hammond, (ed.), *The Sacred in a Secular Age* (1985). Thus one can compare the Cathars of the twelfth century, who rejected much of the Christian faith but based a great deal of their practice upon Christian monasticism, and the more recent 'religions' created by such beliefs as Feng Shui.
49. The Board of Mission Report, *The Search for Faith* (1996).
50. This was suggested by Marie Coleman Nelson in *The Narcissistic Condition* (1977) after her work with Zen Buddhists, the Divine Light Mission and the Meher Baba Movement.

CHAPTER 3: *Renewal in the Temple*

1. It was only during the persecution by Nero in AD 64 that the Roman authorities distinguished between Jews and Christians and declared that therefore the Christians were not covered by the dispensation given to the Jews by Augustus and Claudius. It is even possible that it was the trial of Paul in 62 which led to this decision: cf. Robin Lane Fox, *Pagans and Christians* (1986). It was only as the Christian movement became potentially powerful that it was noticed by the authorities.
2. Gerd Theissen, *The Social Setting of Pauline Christianity* (1982).
3. For Luke this is so important that he puts it as the first incident he records in Jesus' public ministry (Luke 4:16–30). Mark and Matthew record it later and in much less detail (Mark 6:1–6; Matt. 13:54–58).
4. 'Luke's references to the Spirit in the inauguration narrative signify that from his baptism to his ascension the entire ministry of Jesus is charismatic': R. Stronstad, *The Charismatic Theology of St Luke* (1984).
5. It was for this reason that the charge that he 'ate with tax-collectors' – widely regarded as collaborators – was particularly dangerous, as was the challenge about tax (Mark 12:13–17). He was seen as not sufficiently xenophobic.
6. Bosch, *Transforming Mission*.
7. Gird Theissen, *The First Followers of Jesus* (1981).

8. Stronstad, *The Charismatic Theology of St Luke.*
9. There is uncertainty as to their identity. Possibly they were the emancipated Jews of different nationalities expelled from Rome, who are mentioned by Tacitus. It is noteworthy that, on any reading, they were themselves outsiders. Because of this the synagogue would have been their focal cultural centre to a much greater extent than it would have been to the ordinary citizens of Jerusalem.
10. There may, of course, be political as well as historical reasons why Luke recorded those incidents which showed the authorities in a good light.
11. Whether the original writer of Revelation intended to identify Babylon with Rome is uncertain but it was a commonplace of Christian thinking by the second century.
12. Tacitus, writing fifty years later, did not believe the truth of the accusations of arson which had been brought against the Christians in Rome, but saw nothing much wrong in the execution of some members of a group 'hated for their vices'. These were popularly believed to be incest and cannibalism.
13. Revelation 17:6.
14. The long list of people in Romans 16 must have been known not only to Paul but also to at least some of the recipients of the letter.
15. Colossians 1:29.
16. E.g. Romans 6:17. It was not restricted just to the whole body of apostolic teaching. It also referred to the teachings of the Pharisees, the Nicholaitans and even Baalam (Revelation 2:14).
17. E.g. in Luke 15:20. It came to this developed meaning via the Septuagint which used it to denote the seat of emotions in the stomach (in the same way as we use the word 'heart').
18. Didache 15:1 This passage is probably later than some of the earlier sections of the Didache and well illustrates the transition from an itinerant to a settled ministry. Like much of the Didache it is almost impossible to date with accuracy.
19. Here *time* – 'price', 'honour' – almost certainly refers to a double honorarium.
20. Margaret MacDonald, *The Pauline Churches: A Socio-historical Study of Institutionalisation in the Pauline and deutero-Pauline writings* (1988).
21. C. Rowland, *Christian Origins* (1985).
22. See, for example, Von Campenhousen, 'it is love which is the true organising and unifying force within the Church, and which creates in her a paradoxical form of order diametrically opposed to all natural systems of organisations': *Ecclesiastical Authority and Spiritual Power in the Church of the First Three Centuries* (1962).
23. Just as in the eighth century Boniface was called the 'Apostle to the Germans' and Willibrord of York was 'Apostle to the Frisians'.
24. *Episkopos* is occasionally used in secular literature and the Septuagint for religious officials, but only for those having responsibility for buildings or money rather than liturgical or spiritual oversight.
25. Modern theories of 'apostolic succession' do not appear in Irenaeus – and his list is almost certainly make-believe before Bishop Sixtus.
26. The canon of both Old and New Testaments as we have it today was finally agreed by a Council in 382. The Council also asked Jerome to revise the text.
27. Van der Aalst (trans. David Bosch), *Aantekeningen bij de hellenisering van het christendom* (1974).
28. Christopher Rowland, *Christian Origins* (1985).

29. The other movements which might possibly claim this title are the gnostics and the Marcionites. However, both of them were severely reductionist: the gnostics had an other-worldly faith which speculated that the creation had not been the work of God, but of an imperfect Demiurge, and Marcion preached a simplistic God of Love (and excluded the whole of the Old Testament and all the gospels except an expurgated version of Luke).

30. Like many a convert he was an enthusiast – he wanted disciplinary questions to be decided by a board of prophets. He wrote *Seven Books against the Church in Defence of Montanism* (now lost).

31. Christine Trevett, *Montanism* (1996).

32. The word 'heathen' has the same connotation: it is an Old English word meaning 'dweller on the heath', i.e. 'a backwoodsman'.

33. The Montanists held that Eve was honoured by God as she was the first person who tasted of the tree of the knowledge of good and evil.

34. It is noticeable that the orthodox did not deny the reality of prophecy and it seems to have been encountered in non-Montanist circles, though it became rarer, possibly in reaction to what were perceived as Montanist excesses.

35. Acts 10:14.

36. Acts 15:1.

37. Acts 15:30.

38. While their 'Gospel of Matthew' may be the canonical book, it might also be some modification of it or even a conflation of all the gospels, selected to suit their theology.

39. Possibly the less extreme group were called Nazarenes. The whole subject is murky since the Ebionites are known almost entirely through the writings of their enemies.

40. The internet reveals that there is a modern American group which has adopted Ebionite theology and practices!

41. Justin may have had a particular interest in the subject because he was born in Samaria at the ancient city of Shechem.

42. A study of this subject is particularly important because of the present multiplication of cultures within one culture: e.g. youth culture, withdrawal culture. Each of these have their different outlooks and lifestyles within one overarching 'Western culture'; like ice-floes in a turbulent sea they clash where their boundaries meet.

43. MacDonald, *The Pauline Churches*.

44. This is also well illustrated by the divergence between the Eastern and Western Churches which led to the Schism of 1054, where the disharmonies which arose between Byzantine and Roman cultures were reflected in ecclesiastical authority and theology. The defining issue was the 'filioque clause' but there were also a multitude of cultural, political and theological differences.

45. Millennial sects which predict the imminent end of the world try to prevent this process by saying that time is nearly at an end, so there is no opportunity to accommodate to the culture.

46. Galatians 5:13.

CHAPTER 4: *Renewal in the Cloister*

1. To be distinguished from the three kinds of Celtic pilgrimage outlined in the Irish Book of Lismore as: (a) a useless wandering, (b) those who could not go on pilgrimage because of home responsibilities, and (c) those who left their country for God's sake.

2. Those monasteries with a Celtic background soon fell victim to this tendency because abbots chose their own successors. The Benedictine model where abbots were elected remained independent, but chicanery and heavy-handed pressure from the lay authorities brought them into line.

3. This was an eighth-century systematisation of the original Rule of Benedict.

4. These were not entirely unique to Cluny. Other founders had begun to incorporate similar rules. Where Cluny was unique was in its degree of access to the Popes and the use of their support.

5. C. H. Lawrence, *Mediaeval Monasticism* (1989). The reigns of the four most prominent abbots spanned nearly two centuries: Odo (926–944), Mayeul (965–994), Odilo (994–1048) and Hugh (1049–1109).

6. Some entire orders put themselves under the oversight of Cluny. Thus La Charité brought 70 dependent monasteries with them.

7. The Abbot of Bury St Edmunds had to provide a permanent garrison of ten knights in Norwich.

8. The abbots were often turned to for advice and diplomatic expertise. Odilo was on terms with many crowned heads and Hugh was a confidante of Emperor Henry III and helped to broker the historic meeting between the pope and the emperor-elect at Canossa in 1077. Several Cluniacs became popes and archbishops.

9. From *Peter the Venerable vs. St Bernard of Clairvaux*: Internet Medieval Sourcebook.

10. The original foundation, high in the Alps, was swept by an avalanche and several brothers were killed. This forced a retreat to the lower slopes at Grande Chartreuse.

11. The austerity of their life meant that they had few followers and even the Grande Chartreuse had only 13 monks and 16 lay brothers: as its founder St Bruno said, 'the sons of contemplation are fewer than the sons of action'. However, it can be said that the Carthusian is the only order which has not at some time degenerated and required reform.

12. Cluny had been used by popes from its earliest days, but in 1024 this was regularised and all Cluniac monks were put directly under the authority of the pope. The local bishop counted for nothing.

13. One example was Roland Allen, a missionary who had to come back home within a few years and whose classic book, *Missionary Methods: St Paul's or Ours?*, is still in print seventy years after he wrote it. His message only really began to be heard in the 1980s.

14. Many renewals have a desire for impressive headquarters and freehold property. Perhaps these things denote permanence and the 'arrival' of the renewal. I have suggested to many involved in renewals that property ties down what should be light-footed. If it is necessary then leasehold is more flexible than freehold.

15. 'The Devil's Distortion' is a private paper.

16. Matthew 22:29.

17. John 12:24.

CHAPTER 5: *Renewal in the Church*

1. It was noteworthy that the definitions became increasingly precise, from the Lutherans at Augsburg in 1530 and the Council of Trent (1545–63) to the French in 1559 and the Belgic Confession of 1561. Christians were increasingly taught to regard others as heretics. Thus for the Lutheran Philip Nicolai the three great enemies of the faith were the Turks, the papacy and Calvinism.

2. Charles Williams, *The Descent of the Dove* (1950).
3. The numbers burnt at the stake are often exaggerated. It was probably no higher than 3000.
4. This was not the first Index. Henry VIII issued a list of prohibited books in 1529. It was a vain attempt to stem the tide – by 1500 there were 1700 presses throughout Europe.
5. Richard Neibuhr, *The Churches of the Disinherited* (1929). He goes on to blame the leaders of the Reformation for failing to meet these needs and thus leading to the Anabaptists and the Peasants' War.
6. Papal claims became extreme and even blasphemous in the nineteenth century, with Pius IX being sometimes described as 'The Word Incarnate still dwelling among us'. Even as late as 1958, just before Vatican II, Pius XII echoed the claim that the Roman Catholic Church was 'one flock under one supreme shepherd. This is the doctrine of the Catholic truth from whom no one may digress without ruining his or her faith as well as salvation'. Pope Paul VI, when told that this is a barrier to unity, mournfully said, 'But what can we do?' Modern communication and the influence of papal nuncios has helped the centripetal forces in the Roman Catholic Church.
7. A movement in the fourteenth and fifteenth centuries which had Bishop Grosseteste of Lincoln as one of its leaders.
8. An unsuccessful attempt was made to link religion and science by the Hermetic philosophy, a curious amalgam of mystical and even magical alchemy. The great poet (and Welsh doctor), Henry Vaughan (1622–95) was a believer.
9. Kenneth Hylson-Smith, *The Churches in England from Elizabeth I to Elizabeth II* (1998) well shows how the English Reformation was the work of a comparatively small number of people.
10. Owen Chadwick, *The Reformation* (1964).
11. Cf. Martin D.W. Jones, *The Counter Revolution: Religion and Society in Early Modern Europe* (1999).
12. It has been estimated that in his ten years of missionary work he brought 700,000 people to Christ. Needless to say such a figure cannot be either denied or confirmed.
13. The largest number were in Nagasaki. The second atomic bomb wiped out the largest concentration of Christians in Japan.
14. Thus Ricci learned Chinese, mastered the classic Confucian texts, dressed as a mandarin, joined the imperial court – and produced a map of China which was the standard for many years.
15. At the time of the condemnation the Jesuits had fallen into papal disfavour and they were suppressed in 1773. The profusion of Chinese and Japanese texts and works of art sent back by the missionaries which are still in the Vatican testify to this period.
16. Bosch, *Transforming Mission*.
17. The place of the wanderer for Christ is important in any study of Christian mission. The Celtic monks were *perigrinati* who wandered over Europe, and the friars of medieval times were similarly footloose. The Celts were heartily condemned by the more stationary Benedictines and the friars by their outraged ecclesiastical contemporaries – except the popes who encouraged them. His crossing of boundaries was the chief accusation against George Whitefield in eighteenth-century America.
18. Similar outbreaks of charismatic phenomena were not unknown among German pietists: they were called 'inspired congregations'.

19. It is particularly noteworthy how quickly the New Churches have evolved from having a group of co-equal elders, to the need for a 'pastor', and then for an 'apostle' from outside the church.

20. This also applies to local churches and their need to think outside the boundaries of the congregation ('They are not our members'), the boundaries of expectation ('They will never respond') and the boundaries of church life ('They are not our sort').

21. There have been modern attempts to portray these faiths as mainly peace-loving. However recent research shows that even the supposedly peace-loving Maya people practised extensive human sacrifice.

22. A study of Victorian missionary booklets challenging Christians to consider work overseas shows that the adventure of striding through the unknown was seen as a powerful motivation. In tune with the current colonial expansion the challenge was to colonise for Christ.

CHAPTER 6: *Renewal Goes West*

1. Born in 1703, he died in 1758 as the result of one of the earliest smallpox inoculations, which went wrong.

2. In this chapter we shall use 'revival' in its American sense of an outbreak of religious fervour which may well be organised beforehand (the term was coined at the time of the Awakenings). This is usually closer in meaning to the way we have used the word 'renewal' rather than 'revival', based on the definitions given in the Introduction.

3. Different authors give different figures but it was certainly extremely low at the time of the American Revolution. This was not confined to America. In 1820 only 7.2% of adults were Easter communicants in the Church of England; on Easter Day in 1800 there were only 6 communicants in St Paul's Cathedral.

4. Cf. Jon Butler's *Enthusiasm Described and Decried: the Great Awakening as Interpretative Fiction* (1995), which says it was merely 'a short-lived Calvinist revival in New England during the early 1740s'. Certainly it sometimes acquired mythical proportions in the stories told by revivalist preachers.

5. I.e. from 17% to 34%. It continued to increase until it reached 62% in 1980.

6. Revelation 20: 4,5,7. The statement that those who are to reign with Christ are those who have been 'beheaded' (literally 'killed with an axe') is usually either ignored or spiritualised away by millennialists. James Moorhead in *The Erosion of Postmillennialism in American Religious Thought* describes the passage as 'simultaneously canonical and obscure'.

7. The idea of a sabbath of 1000 years is also spoken of in 2 Enoch 32:2ff. but with no messianic reference.

8. Psalm 10:1 – the thought is a constant refrain in the psalter.

9. Calvin's idea may have come, via the Franciscans, from Joachim di Fiori (c.1135–1202) who postulated the theory of the Age of the Father (the Old Testament era), the Age of the Son (the New Testament period and 42 generations after) and the Age of the Spirit (which had just dawned) which would lead to the conversion of the world.

10. The American Board 1813.

11. As David Bosch says in *Transforming Mission*, 'God and humans were reconciled by deifying the latter and humanising the former'.

12. Israel is central to much pre-millennial thinking and this has led to an uncritical support for the modern state of Israel.

13. Thus Charles Finney insisted that Oberlin College, which he joined as

Professor of Systematic Theology, should admit blacks – a radical idea for 1835.

14. Only John and Charles Wesley and some Methodists had taken the step of being prepared to be known as Arminians. It led to their break with George Whitefield.

15. This happened at the same time in Britain as dispensationalism became fashionable in evangelical circles through the Plymouth Brethren and the Scofield Bible.

16. The issue is far from settled. There has been something of a swing back to post-millennialism but it caused such friction in Fuller Seminary in the 1960s that the college almost disintegrated: cf. George Marsden *Reforming Fundamentalism: Fuller Seminary and the New Evangelicalism* (1987).

17. These circuit riders covered vast distances in constant danger from weather and Indian attack. Of the first 700 riders half died before they were thirty. Cartwright survived his experiences, wrote *The Autobiography of Peter Cartwright* and died aged 87.

18. Roger Finke and Rodney Stark, *The Churching of America 1776–1990* (1992). The thrust of the book, backed by many statistics, is that as American churches have 'modernised their doctrines and embraced temporal values they have gone into decline'.

19. 'Voluntaryism' is sometimes confused with 'voluntarism' – the philosophical view that the will is of greater significance than other mental faculties.

20. George Marsden, *Fundamentalism and American Culture. The Shaping of Twentieth-century Evangelicalism: 1870–1925* (1980).

21. It is noteworthy how many of these sects had women either as founders or as the main energisers. When old churches denied them a role they found an outlet in the new.

22. Richard Niebuhr, *The Kingdom of God in America* (1959).

23. In *Dynamics of Spiritual Life* (1979)

24. A most vivid personal memory was having to step at the last minute very inadequately into David Watson's shoes in 1984 when he became ill. He had agreed to lead a mission south of Los Angeles, but only on the understanding that it would be genuinely ecumenical. It was the first time such a thing had ever happened in California. I contrasted it with England where such events were commonplace.

25. The internet is a rich library of these crazed ideas, and is also the medium through which they are spread all too widely.

26. Many of the early Congregationalists (and some Presbyterians) taught that Arius was a trustworthy authority in the Church whose truths had been crushed by orthodoxy.

27. Many of the controversies of the nineteenth and early twentieth centuries concerned the leadership and the teaching given in denominational seminaries.

28. The early Pentecostal renewals at Azuza Street in 1906 tried to 'leave it to the Spirit' and refused to advertise. However it was found to be chaotic and the policy was changed.

29. It can be well seen in the expanding number of missionary societies in the US. By 1900 there were 81; by 1939 there were 228; by 1980 there were 706.

30. All the quotations are from Jonathan Edwards, *Thoughts on the Revival in New England*.

31. The classic passage is 1 Corinthians 12–14. 1 Corinthians 13 is a vital

element in Paul's argument for here he describes the attitude of *agape* which should pervade the exercise of the gifts.

CHAPTER 7: *Renewal in Today's World*

1. Isaiah 24:18, 19, 23.
2. Deuteronomy 27:17.
3. Many people claim to have been the first users of the term. Arnold Toynbee certainly used it in 1946.
4. 'Post-modernism is a convenient label, not an organised movement, nor does it amount to a coherent ideology': Richard Evans, *In Defence of History* (1997).
5. The titles of the sections in this chapter are adapted from Yvonne Craig's contribution to *Tomorrow is another Country* (1996).
6. Acts 17:21. Much modern evangelism is Athenian – introducing people to the 'Unknown God' (*Agnosto Theo*) whom they already know and giving them a name for him.
7. *Good News People* (1999). This also showed that this attitude was contrary to the New Testament definition of an evangelist, and was not a true description of the great majority of those who were recognised as such.
8. Hence it is often replaced by 'spiritual guide', 'soul friend' or the Celtic word 'anamchara'.
9. In *In Defence of History* (1997).
10. Deconstructionism therefore gives a spurious academic validity to Holocaust denial.
11. Professor Graham Holderness in commenting on Shakespeare's *Richard III*.
12. Simon Reynolds, *Energy Flash* (1998).
13. Different narratives of the same events such as the gospels and parts of the Old Testament are *very* post-modern: cf. post-modern novels like *The Name of the Rose* and *The French Lieutenant's Woman*.
14. Martin E. Marty and R. Scott Appleby, *The Glory and the Power: The Fundamentalist Challenge to the Modern World* (1992).
15. Song called 'High Hopes' by Pink Floyd; quoted in *The Search for Faith* (1996).

CHAPTER 8: *The Hypothesis Reviewed*

1. 1 Peter 3:8f.
2. Collect for Whit Sunday in the Book of Common Prayer. It is the New Testament gift of *diakrisis* – 'discernment': cf. Hebrews 5:14: 'solid food is for the mature, for those whose faculties have been trained by practice to distinguish good from evil'. There are few spiritual gifts more necessary for a Christian leader.
3. Colossians 3:12.
4. The handling of the charismatic movement by the Presbyterian Church in the United States during the 1970s and 1980s is particularly instructive, moving from a tone of bewilderment and outright condemnation to a more understanding and conciliatory tone.
5. John 7:51,52; 19:39. (John is probably indicating, in his usual sideways way, that this was a royal burial. Old Testament kings were buried with an abundance of spices: cf. 2 Chronicles 16:14.)
6. Acts 5:33–39.
7. Thomas A. Smail, *The Forgotten Father* (Hodder & Stoughton, 1980).

CHAPTER 9: *Does the Splendour* Have *to Fade?*
1. Luke 8:14.
2. 1 Corinthians 15:37.
3. St Simon (c.390–459) began with a low pillar and then built it higher and higher in order to get further away from people, ending up at about forty feet. He was widely imitated by other Stylites up to the tenth century and even later. They sometimes had a hut on top of their pillar.
4. Jeremiah 7:24 puts it well: 'In the stubborness of their evil will, they walked in their own counsels and looked backward rather than forward'.

Index